50 Game Day Snack Recipes for Home

By: Kelly Johnson

Table of Contents

- Buffalo Chicken Dip
- Cheesy Bacon Jalapeño Poppers
- Spinach Artichoke Dip
- Loaded Nachos
- BBQ Meatballs
- Mini Corn Dogs
- Chicken Wings
- Stuffed Mushrooms
- Guacamole
- Queso Dip
- Pigs in a Blanket
- Sliders
- Cheese Ball
- Deviled Eggs
- Pretzel Bites
- Chili Cheese Fries
- Mozzarella Sticks
- Potato Skins
- Onion Rings
- Pizza Rolls
- Garlic Knots
- Shrimp Cocktail
- Chicken Taquitos
- Salsa
- Spinach Dip
- Ham and Cheese Sliders
- Beef Empanadas
- Sweet and Spicy Nuts
- Popcorn
- Stuffed Peppers
- Chicken Tenders
- Mac and Cheese Bites
- Sausage Balls
- Jalapeño Poppers
- Tater Tots

- Chocolate Covered Pretzels
- Fruit Platter
- Veggie Platter
- Cheese and Crackers
- Chicken Quesadillas
- Meat and Cheese Platter
- Hummus
- Roasted Chickpeas
- Fried Pickles
- Baked Zucchini Chips
- Soft Pretzels
- Caprese Skewers
- Chicken Satay
- Greek Yogurt Dip
- Bacon-Wrapped Dates

Buffalo Chicken Dip

Ingredients:

- 2 cups shredded cooked chicken (rotisserie chicken works great)
- 8 oz cream cheese, softened
- 1/2 cup sour cream
- 1/2 cup ranch dressing
- 1/2 cup Buffalo wing sauce (such as Frank's RedHot)
- 1 cup shredded cheddar cheese (plus extra for topping)
- 1/2 cup blue cheese crumbles (optional)
- Sliced green onions or chopped parsley, for garnish (optional)
- Tortilla chips, celery sticks, and carrot sticks, for serving

Instructions:

1. Preheat the Oven:
    - Preheat your oven to 350°F (175°C).
2. Prepare the Dip:
    - In a large mixing bowl, combine the softened cream cheese, sour cream, ranch dressing, and Buffalo wing sauce. Mix until smooth and well combined.
    - Fold in the shredded chicken, shredded cheddar cheese, and blue cheese crumbles (if using).
3. Bake the Dip:
    - Transfer the mixture to a baking dish or oven-safe skillet.
    - Spread the mixture evenly and sprinkle a little extra shredded cheddar cheese on top.
    - Bake in the preheated oven for 20-25 minutes, or until the dip is hot and bubbly.
4. Garnish and Serve:
    - Remove the dip from the oven and let it cool slightly.
    - Garnish with sliced green onions or chopped parsley, if desired.
    - Serve warm with tortilla chips, celery sticks, and carrot sticks for dipping.

Tips:

- Chicken: Rotisserie chicken is a convenient option, but you can also use any leftover cooked chicken or quickly poach some chicken breasts and shred them.
- Spice Level: Adjust the amount of Buffalo wing sauce to your taste. Add more for extra heat or reduce for a milder dip.
- Make-Ahead: You can prepare the dip up to a day in advance. Assemble the dip, cover, and refrigerate until ready to bake. You may need to add a few extra minutes to the baking time if baking straight from the refrigerator.

Buffalo chicken dip is a creamy, tangy, and spicy appetizer that's always a hit. Enjoy it with your favorite dippers and watch it disappear quickly!

Cheesy Bacon Jalapeño Poppers

Ingredients:

- 12 large jalapeño peppers
- 8 oz cream cheese, softened
- 1 cup shredded cheddar cheese
- 1/2 cup shredded mozzarella cheese
- 1/2 teaspoon garlic powder
- 1/2 teaspoon onion powder
- Salt and pepper, to taste
- 12 slices bacon, cut in half
- Fresh chives or parsley, chopped, for garnish (optional)

Instructions:

1. Prepare the Jalapeños:
    - Preheat your oven to 400°F (200°C).
    - Slice each jalapeño in half lengthwise and remove the seeds and membranes. If you prefer less heat, remove all seeds and membranes thoroughly.
2. Make the Cheese Filling:
    - In a medium bowl, combine the softened cream cheese, shredded cheddar cheese, shredded mozzarella cheese, garlic powder, onion powder, salt, and pepper. Mix until well combined.
3. Fill the Jalapeños:
    - Spoon the cheese mixture into each jalapeño half, filling them generously.
4. Wrap with Bacon:
    - Wrap each filled jalapeño half with a half slice of bacon, securing with a toothpick if necessary.
5. Bake the Poppers:
    - Place the bacon-wrapped jalapeño poppers on a baking sheet lined with parchment paper or a baking rack.
    - Bake in the preheated oven for 20-25 minutes, or until the bacon is crispy and the cheese filling is bubbly.
6. Serve:
    - Remove the poppers from the oven and let them cool slightly.
    - Garnish with chopped fresh chives or parsley, if desired.
    - Serve warm.

Tips:

- Handling Jalapeños: Wear gloves while handling and seeding the jalapeños to avoid getting the spicy oils on your skin, which can cause irritation.

- Bacon: Thinner bacon works best for wrapping as it crisps up nicely. If using thick-cut bacon, you may need to bake the poppers a bit longer or partially cook the bacon before wrapping.
- Grilling Option: For an added smoky flavor, grill the jalapeño poppers over medium heat for about 10-15 minutes, turning occasionally until the bacon is crispy and the filling is melted.

Cheesy bacon jalapeño poppers are always a hit at parties and gatherings. They're the perfect combination of spicy, creamy, and savory, making them an irresistible treat for any occasion!

Spinach Artichoke Dip

Ingredients:

- 1 (10 oz) package frozen chopped spinach, thawed and drained
- 1 (14 oz) can artichoke hearts, drained and chopped
- 8 oz cream cheese, softened
- 1/2 cup sour cream
- 1/4 cup mayonnaise
- 1/2 cup grated Parmesan cheese
- 1 cup shredded mozzarella cheese
- 2 cloves garlic, minced
- Salt and pepper, to taste
- Optional: A pinch of red pepper flakes for a bit of heat

Instructions:

1. Preheat the Oven:
   - Preheat your oven to 350°F (175°C).
2. Prepare the Spinach and Artichokes:
   - Make sure the spinach is well-drained by squeezing out any excess moisture with your hands or using a clean kitchen towel.
   - Chop the artichoke hearts into small pieces.
3. Mix the Ingredients:
   - In a large bowl, combine the softened cream cheese, sour cream, and mayonnaise. Mix until smooth and creamy.
   - Add the grated Parmesan cheese, shredded mozzarella cheese, minced garlic, and chopped artichokes. Mix well.
   - Fold in the drained spinach until all ingredients are well combined.
   - Season with salt, pepper, and red pepper flakes (if using) to taste.
4. Bake the Dip:
   - Transfer the mixture to a baking dish or oven-safe skillet.
   - Smooth the top with a spatula and sprinkle a little extra shredded mozzarella cheese on top for a golden, bubbly finish.
   - Bake in the preheated oven for 25-30 minutes, or until the dip is hot and bubbly, and the top is lightly golden.
5. Serve:
   - Remove from the oven and let it cool slightly before serving.
   - Serve warm with your choice of dippers such as tortilla chips, pita chips, sliced baguette, or fresh vegetables.

Tips:

- Fresh Spinach Option: You can use fresh spinach instead of frozen. Sauté about 10-12 ounces of fresh spinach in a little olive oil until wilted, then chop and proceed with the recipe.
- Cheese Variations: Feel free to experiment with different cheeses such as Gruyère or fontina for added flavor.
- Make-Ahead: You can prepare the dip up to a day in advance. Assemble the dip, cover, and refrigerate until ready to bake. You may need to add a few extra minutes to the baking time if baking straight from the refrigerator.

Spinach artichoke dip is a creamy, cheesy, and flavorful appetizer that's always a hit. Enjoy it warm with your favorite dippers and watch it disappear quickly!

Loaded Nachos

Ingredients:

- Tortilla chips
- 1 lb ground beef, chicken, or turkey
- 1 packet taco seasoning (or homemade taco seasoning)
- 1 cup black beans, rinsed and drained
- 1 cup corn kernels (fresh, frozen, or canned)
- 2 cups shredded cheese (cheddar, Monterey Jack, or a blend)
- 1/2 cup diced tomatoes
- 1/2 cup diced red onion
- 1-2 jalapeños, sliced (optional)
- 1/4 cup sliced black olives (optional)
- 1/4 cup chopped cilantro (optional)

For Serving:

- Sour cream
- Guacamole
- Salsa or pico de gallo
- Sliced green onions
- Lime wedges

Instructions:

1. **Prepare the Meat:**
    - In a large skillet, cook the ground meat over medium heat until browned and fully cooked. Drain any excess fat.
    - Add the taco seasoning and a little water according to the seasoning packet instructions. Simmer for a few minutes until the sauce thickens and coats the meat.
2. **Preheat the Oven:**
    - Preheat your oven to 400°F (200°C).
3. **Assemble the Nachos:**
    - On a large baking sheet or oven-safe platter, spread out a layer of tortilla chips.
    - Evenly distribute the cooked meat over the chips.
    - Sprinkle black beans and corn over the meat.
    - Top with shredded cheese, ensuring even coverage.
4. **Bake the Nachos:**
    - Place the nachos in the preheated oven and bake for 8-10 minutes, or until the cheese is melted and bubbly.
5. **Add Fresh Toppings:**
    - Remove the nachos from the oven.

- Sprinkle diced tomatoes, diced red onions, sliced jalapeños, sliced black olives, and chopped cilantro over the top.
6. Serve:
    - Serve the loaded nachos immediately with sides of sour cream, guacamole, salsa or pico de gallo, and sliced green onions.
    - Garnish with lime wedges for an extra burst of flavor.

Tips:

- Layering: For extra cheesy nachos, you can layer the chips, cheese, and toppings in multiple layers before baking.
- Protein Options: Substitute the ground meat with shredded rotisserie chicken, pulled pork, or even a meatless ground beef substitute for a vegetarian option.
- Customizable: Loaded nachos are highly customizable. Add or omit ingredients based on your preferences, such as bell peppers, avocado, or hot sauce.

Loaded nachos are a crowd-pleaser and can be tailored to suit your taste. Enjoy this delicious and fun dish with your favorite toppings and accompaniments!

BBQ Meatballs

Ingredients:

For the Meatballs:

- 1 lb ground beef
- 1/2 cup breadcrumbs
- 1/4 cup milk
- 1 egg
- 1/4 cup finely chopped onion
- 2 cloves garlic, minced
- 1/4 cup grated Parmesan cheese
- 1 tablespoon Worcestershire sauce
- 1 teaspoon salt
- 1/2 teaspoon black pepper
- 1/2 teaspoon smoked paprika

For the BBQ Sauce:

- 1 cup barbecue sauce (homemade or store-bought)
- 1/2 cup ketchup
- 1/4 cup brown sugar
- 1 tablespoon apple cider vinegar
- 1 tablespoon Worcestershire sauce
- 1 teaspoon smoked paprika
- 1/2 teaspoon garlic powder
- 1/2 teaspoon onion powder

Instructions:

1. Preheat the Oven:
    - Preheat your oven to 400°F (200°C). Line a baking sheet with parchment paper or lightly grease it.
2. Prepare the Meatballs:
    - In a large bowl, combine the breadcrumbs and milk. Let it sit for a few minutes to allow the breadcrumbs to absorb the milk.
    - Add the ground beef, egg, finely chopped onion, minced garlic, grated Parmesan cheese, Worcestershire sauce, salt, black pepper, and smoked paprika to the breadcrumb mixture. Mix until well combined.
    - Shape the mixture into 1-inch meatballs and place them on the prepared baking sheet.
3. Bake the Meatballs:
    - Bake in the preheated oven for 15-20 minutes, or until the meatballs are cooked through and lightly browned.

4. Prepare the BBQ Sauce:
    - While the meatballs are baking, combine the barbecue sauce, ketchup, brown sugar, apple cider vinegar, Worcestershire sauce, smoked paprika, garlic powder, and onion powder in a medium saucepan.
    - Bring the mixture to a simmer over medium heat, stirring occasionally. Reduce the heat to low and let it simmer for about 10 minutes to allow the flavors to meld.
5. Combine Meatballs and Sauce:
    - Once the meatballs are done, transfer them to the saucepan with the BBQ sauce. Gently stir to coat the meatballs in the sauce.
    - Let the meatballs simmer in the sauce for about 5-10 minutes, allowing them to absorb the flavors.
6. Serve:
    - Transfer the BBQ meatballs to a serving dish and garnish with chopped fresh parsley or green onions if desired.
    - Serve hot with toothpicks for easy grabbing, or as a main dish with rice or mashed potatoes.

Tips:

- Make-Ahead: You can make the meatballs ahead of time and freeze them. Simply reheat and toss them in the BBQ sauce when ready to serve.
- Slow Cooker Option: After baking the meatballs, transfer them to a slow cooker. Pour the BBQ sauce over the meatballs and cook on low for 2-3 hours.
- Flavor Variations: Experiment with different BBQ sauces to change up the flavor profile, such as spicy, smoky, or tangy BBQ sauces.

BBQ meatballs are a delicious and versatile dish that's sure to be a hit at any gathering. Enjoy their savory, sweet, and tangy flavors!

Mini Corn Dogs

Ingredients:

For the Corn Dogs:

- 1 cup yellow cornmeal
- 1 cup all-purpose flour
- 1/4 cup granulated sugar
- 1 tablespoon baking powder
- 1/2 teaspoon salt
- 1 cup milk
- 1 large egg
- 2 tablespoons vegetable oil
- 12 hot dogs (or mini sausages)
- Wooden skewers or toothpicks (if using full-size hot dogs, cut them in half)

For Frying:

- Vegetable oil, for frying

Instructions:

1. Prepare the Hot Dogs:
    - Pat the hot dogs dry with paper towels.
    - Insert wooden skewers or toothpicks into each hot dog, leaving enough of the stick exposed to hold the corn dog.
2. Make the Batter:
    - In a large bowl, whisk together the cornmeal, flour, sugar, baking powder, and salt.
    - In a separate bowl, whisk together the milk, egg, and vegetable oil.
    - Pour the wet ingredients into the dry ingredients and stir until just combined. The batter should be thick but smooth.
3. Heat the Oil:
    - Pour vegetable oil into a large pot or deep fryer to a depth of about 2-3 inches. Heat the oil to 350°F (175°C).
4. Coat the Hot Dogs:
    - Pour the batter into a tall glass or container that will allow you to dip the hot dogs easily.
    - Dip each hot dog into the batter, coating it completely. You can use a spoon to help coat the hot dogs evenly.
    - Allow any excess batter to drip off before frying.
5. Fry the Corn Dogs:
    - Carefully place the coated hot dogs into the hot oil. Fry in batches, making sure not to overcrowd the pot.

- Fry the mini corn dogs for about 2-3 minutes, or until golden brown and crispy. Turn them occasionally to ensure even cooking.
  - Use a slotted spoon or tongs to remove the corn dogs from the oil and place them on a plate lined with paper towels to drain any excess oil.
6. Serve:
  - Serve the mini corn dogs hot with your favorite dipping sauces such as ketchup, mustard, or honey mustard.

Tips:

- Dry the Hot Dogs: Ensure the hot dogs are thoroughly dry before dipping them in the batter to help the batter adhere better.
- Consistent Temperature: Maintain the oil temperature at 350°F for even cooking. If the oil is too hot, the batter will burn before the hot dog is cooked through; if it's too cool, the batter will absorb more oil and become greasy.
- Batter Consistency: The batter should be thick enough to coat the hot dogs without dripping off too quickly. If it's too thin, add a bit more flour; if too thick, add a little more milk.

Mini corn dogs are a delightful treat that everyone will love. Enjoy them fresh and hot with your favorite condiments!

Chicken Wings

Ingredients:

For the Wings:

- 2 lbs chicken wings (wingettes and drumettes)
- 2 tablespoons vegetable oil
- 1 teaspoon salt
- 1 teaspoon black pepper
- 1 teaspoon garlic powder
- 1 teaspoon paprika
- 1/2 teaspoon onion powder
- 1/2 teaspoon baking powder (for extra crispiness)

For the Buffalo Sauce:

- 1/2 cup hot sauce (such as Frank's RedHot)
- 1/4 cup unsalted butter, melted
- 1 tablespoon honey (optional for a touch of sweetness)
- 1 tablespoon Worcestershire sauce
- 1/2 teaspoon garlic powder

For Serving:

- Ranch or blue cheese dressing
- Celery sticks
- Carrot sticks

Instructions:

1. Preheat the Oven:
    - Preheat your oven to 425°F (220°C). Line a baking sheet with aluminum foil and place a wire rack on top. This will help the wings cook evenly and stay crispy.
2. Prepare the Wings:
    - Pat the chicken wings dry with paper towels. This is crucial for getting them crispy.
    - In a large bowl, toss the wings with vegetable oil, salt, black pepper, garlic powder, paprika, onion powder, and baking powder until well coated.
3. Bake the Wings:
    - Arrange the wings in a single layer on the wire rack, making sure they aren't touching each other.
    - Bake in the preheated oven for 20 minutes, then flip the wings and bake for another 20-25 minutes, or until the wings are golden brown and crispy.
4. Prepare the Buffalo Sauce:

- While the wings are baking, prepare the buffalo sauce. In a small saucepan, combine the hot sauce, melted butter, honey (if using), Worcestershire sauce, and garlic powder. Heat over low heat, stirring occasionally, until the sauce is well combined and heated through.

5. Toss the Wings in Sauce:
   - Once the wings are done baking, transfer them to a large bowl. Pour the buffalo sauce over the wings and toss to coat them evenly.
6. Serve:
   - Transfer the sauced wings to a serving platter.
   - Serve immediately with ranch or blue cheese dressing, celery sticks, and carrot sticks on the side.

Tips:

- **Extra Crispy Wings:** For even crispier wings, you can let the seasoned wings sit uncovered in the refrigerator for an hour before baking. This helps dry out the skin.
- **Grilling Option:** You can also grill the wings over medium-high heat for about 20-25 minutes, turning occasionally until crispy and cooked through.
- **Flavor Variations:** Feel free to experiment with different sauces and seasonings. Some popular variations include BBQ, honey garlic, and teriyaki.

Chicken wings are always a hit, and this method ensures they are crispy and full of flavor. Enjoy your delicious homemade buffalo wings with your favorite dipping sauces and veggies!

Stuffed Mushrooms

Ingredients:

- 24 large white or cremini mushrooms
- 3 tablespoons olive oil, divided
- 1/4 cup finely chopped onion
- 3 cloves garlic, minced
- 1/2 cup breadcrumbs
- 1/4 cup grated Parmesan cheese
- 1/2 cup shredded mozzarella cheese
- 2 tablespoons chopped fresh parsley
- 1/4 teaspoon dried oregano
- 1/4 teaspoon dried thyme
- Salt and black pepper, to taste
- 2 tablespoons melted butter
- Optional: 1/4 cup finely chopped cooked bacon or sausage for added flavor

Instructions:

1. Preheat the Oven:
   - Preheat your oven to 375°F (190°C). Line a baking sheet with parchment paper or lightly grease it.
2. Prepare the Mushrooms:
   - Gently clean the mushrooms with a damp paper towel to remove any dirt. Remove the stems and finely chop them. Set the mushroom caps aside.
3. Make the Filling:
   - Heat 2 tablespoons of olive oil in a skillet over medium heat. Add the chopped onion and cook until softened, about 3-4 minutes.
   - Add the minced garlic and chopped mushroom stems to the skillet. Cook until the mixture is tender and any liquid has evaporated, about 5 minutes.
   - Stir in the breadcrumbs, grated Parmesan cheese, shredded mozzarella cheese, chopped parsley, dried oregano, dried thyme, salt, and black pepper. If using, add the finely chopped cooked bacon or sausage. Mix well to combine.
4. Stuff the Mushrooms:
   - Brush the mushroom caps with the remaining tablespoon of olive oil. Place them on the prepared baking sheet.
   - Spoon the filling into each mushroom cap, pressing gently to ensure the filling is packed in.
5. Bake the Mushrooms:
   - Drizzle the melted butter over the stuffed mushrooms for added richness.
   - Bake in the preheated oven for 20-25 minutes, or until the mushrooms are tender and the tops are golden brown.
6. Serve:

- Remove from the oven and let them cool slightly before serving.
- Garnish with additional chopped parsley if desired.

Tips:

- Variations: Customize the filling with your favorite ingredients, such as spinach, sun-dried tomatoes, or different cheeses like feta or goat cheese.
- Herbs: Fresh herbs can be used in place of dried herbs for a fresher flavor.
- Make Ahead: Stuffed mushrooms can be assembled ahead of time and stored in the refrigerator until ready to bake. This makes them an excellent choice for parties and gatherings.

Stuffed mushrooms are a tasty and elegant appetizer that's sure to impress your guests. Enjoy them warm and savor the delightful blend of flavors and textures!

Guacamole

Ingredients:

- 3 ripe avocados
- 1 lime, juiced (or 2 tablespoons lime juice)
- 1/2 teaspoon salt
- 1/2 teaspoon ground cumin (optional)
- 1/2 teaspoon garlic powder (optional)
- 1 small onion, finely diced
- 1-2 Roma tomatoes, seeded and diced
- 1-2 jalapeño peppers, seeded and finely chopped
- 2-3 tablespoons fresh cilantro, chopped
- Optional: 1 clove garlic, minced
- Optional: 1/4 teaspoon cayenne pepper for extra heat

Instructions:

1. Prepare the Avocados:
   - Cut the avocados in half, remove the pits, and scoop the flesh into a large bowl.
   - Use a fork or a potato masher to mash the avocados to your desired consistency. Some prefer it smooth, while others like it chunky.
2. Add Lime Juice and Seasonings:
   - Add the lime juice, salt, ground cumin (if using), and garlic powder (if using) to the mashed avocados. Mix well to combine.
3. Mix in the Vegetables:
   - Add the finely diced onion, diced tomatoes, chopped jalapeños, chopped cilantro, and minced garlic (if using). Stir gently to combine all the ingredients.
4. Taste and Adjust:
   - Taste the guacamole and adjust the seasoning as needed. You can add more salt, lime juice, or other spices to suit your taste.
   - If you like your guacamole spicier, add a pinch of cayenne pepper or more finely chopped jalapeños.
5. Serve:
   - Transfer the guacamole to a serving bowl.
   - Serve immediately with tortilla chips, pita chips, or fresh vegetable sticks. Guacamole can also be used as a topping for tacos, burritos, and other Mexican dishes.

Tips:

- Ripe Avocados: Ensure the avocados are ripe by gently pressing them. They should yield slightly to pressure but not feel mushy.

- **Prevent Browning:** To prevent the guacamole from browning, press plastic wrap directly onto the surface of the guacamole to minimize air contact. Alternatively, adding an extra squeeze of lime juice can help.
- **Customization:** Feel free to customize your guacamole with additional ingredients like diced mango, roasted corn, or black beans for extra flavor and texture.

Enjoy this fresh and flavorful guacamole with your favorite dippers or as a complement to your meals!

Queso Dip

Ingredients:

- 8 oz (about 2 cups) shredded cheese (Mexican blend, cheddar, or Monterey Jack)
- 1 tablespoon cornstarch
- 1 cup milk (whole milk preferred)
- 1 tablespoon butter
- 1/2 small onion, finely diced
- 1 jalapeño, seeded and finely diced (optional for heat)
- 1 clove garlic, minced
- 1 (10 oz) can diced tomatoes with green chilies, drained
- 1/4 teaspoon ground cumin
- Salt and pepper, to taste
- Chopped cilantro, for garnish (optional)

Instructions:

1. Prepare the Cheese:
    - In a medium bowl, toss the shredded cheese with the cornstarch until the cheese is evenly coated. This helps the cheese melt smoothly without clumping.
2. Cook the Aromatics:
    - In a medium saucepan, melt the butter over medium heat. Add the diced onion and jalapeño (if using) and cook until softened, about 3-4 minutes.
    - Add the minced garlic and cook for another 30 seconds until fragrant.
3. Make the Queso Dip:
    - Pour the milk into the saucepan with the cooked aromatics. Stir and cook until the milk is heated through and just starts to simmer.
4. Add Cheese and Tomatoes:
    - Reduce the heat to low. Gradually add the cheese mixture, stirring constantly until the cheese is melted and the mixture is smooth and creamy.
5. Season and Serve:
    - Stir in the drained diced tomatoes with green chilies and ground cumin. Season with salt and pepper to taste.
    - Continue to cook on low heat for a few more minutes, stirring occasionally, until the dip is heated through and well combined.
    - If the dip becomes too thick, you can add a splash of milk to reach your desired consistency.
6. Garnish and Serve:
    - Transfer the queso dip to a serving bowl or keep warm in a small slow cooker or fondue pot.
    - Garnish with chopped cilantro if desired.
    - Serve immediately with tortilla chips, pretzels, or your favorite dippers.

Tips:

- Customization: Feel free to customize your queso dip by adding cooked ground beef, chorizo, or black beans for extra flavor and texture.
- Consistency: If the queso dip becomes too thick upon cooling, simply reheat gently and stir in a little more milk to thin it out.
- Spice Level: Adjust the heat by adding more or less jalapeño peppers, or by choosing a spicier variety of diced tomatoes with green chilies.

This homemade queso dip is creamy, cheesy, and packed with flavor—a perfect addition to any gathering or game day spread! Enjoy dipping and sharing with friends and family.

Pigs in a Blanket

Ingredients:

- 1 can (8 oz) refrigerated crescent roll dough (or puff pastry, if preferred)
- 24 cocktail-sized sausages (such as mini hot dogs or cocktail wieners)
- Mustard or dipping sauce of your choice, for serving (optional)

Instructions:

1. Preheat the Oven:
    - Preheat your oven according to the instructions on the crescent roll dough package (usually around 375°F or 190°C).
2. Prepare the Dough:
    - If using crescent roll dough, unroll the dough and separate it into triangles along the perforated lines. If using puff pastry, roll it out slightly on a floured surface and cut into strips.
3. Wrap the Sausages:
    - Take each sausage and wrap it in one triangle of crescent roll dough or one strip of puff pastry. Roll the dough around the sausage, leaving the ends exposed or tucking them underneath, depending on your preference.
4. Arrange on Baking Sheet:
    - Place each wrapped sausage seam-side down on an ungreased baking sheet, spacing them evenly apart.
5. Bake:
    - Bake in the preheated oven for about 12-15 minutes, or until the pastry is golden brown and cooked through.
6. Serve:
    - Remove from the oven and let cool slightly before serving.
    - Serve with mustard or your favorite dipping sauce if desired.

Tips:

- Variations: Experiment with different types of sausages or add a slice of cheese inside the dough for extra flavor.
- Make-Ahead: Pigs in a Blanket can be assembled ahead of time and refrigerated until ready to bake. Just pop them in the oven when your guests arrive.
- Freezing: You can also freeze unbaked Pigs in a Blanket. Arrange them on a baking sheet and freeze until firm, then transfer to a freezer bag. When ready to bake, no need to thaw—just bake them a few minutes longer than fresh.

Pigs in a Blanket are always a hit at parties, gatherings, and even as a fun snack for kids. Enjoy these bite-sized delights warm and fresh out of the oven!

Sliders

Ingredients:

For the Beef Patties:

- 1 lb ground beef (preferably 80% lean)
- Salt and pepper, to taste
- 1 tablespoon Worcestershire sauce
- 1 teaspoon garlic powder
- 1 teaspoon onion powder
- 1/2 teaspoon paprika
- Slider buns or dinner rolls, sliced
- Sliced cheese (optional)

For Serving:

- Slider toppings such as lettuce, tomato slices, pickles, etc.
- Condiments such as ketchup, mustard, mayonnaise, etc.

Instructions:

1. Prepare the Beef Patties:
   - In a large bowl, combine the ground beef, salt, pepper, Worcestershire sauce, garlic powder, onion powder, and paprika. Mix gently until well combined, being careful not to overwork the meat.
2. Form Patties:
   - Divide the beef mixture into equal portions and shape them into small patties, slightly larger than the diameter of your slider buns as they will shrink when cooked.
3. Cook Patties:
   - Heat a grill pan, skillet, or outdoor grill over medium-high heat. Cook the beef patties for about 3-4 minutes per side, or until they reach your desired level of doneness. If adding cheese, place a slice of cheese on each patty during the last minute of cooking to melt.
4. Assemble Sliders:
   - Slice the slider buns or dinner rolls in half horizontally.
   - Place a cooked beef patty on the bottom half of each bun.
   - Add your desired toppings such as lettuce, tomato slices, pickles, etc.
   - Spread condiments on the top half of the buns, such as ketchup, mustard, or mayonnaise.
5. Serve:
   - Close each slider with the top half of the bun and secure with toothpicks if needed.
   - Arrange sliders on a platter and serve immediately.

Tips:

- Variations: You can customize sliders with different types of meat (e.g., chicken, turkey), cheeses, and toppings to suit your preferences.
- Make-Ahead: Prepare the beef patties in advance and refrigerate until ready to cook. You can also assemble the sliders ahead of time, wrap them in foil, and heat in the oven just before serving.
- Side Dishes: Serve sliders with side dishes like coleslaw, potato salad, or french fries for a complete meal.

Sliders are versatile and can be adapted to any occasion or taste. Enjoy these mini sandwiches as a delicious and satisfying treat!

Cheese Ball

Ingredients:

- 2 packages (16 oz total) cream cheese, softened
- 2 cups shredded cheddar cheese (sharp or mild, your choice)
- 1/2 cup chopped pecans or walnuts
- 1/4 cup chopped green onions (green parts only)
- 1 tablespoon Worcestershire sauce
- 1 teaspoon garlic powder
- 1/2 teaspoon onion powder
- 1/4 teaspoon paprika
- Salt and black pepper, to taste
- Optional coating:
    - Additional chopped nuts (pecans or walnuts)
    - Chopped fresh parsley
    - Crumbled bacon bits
    - Everything bagel seasoning

Instructions:

1. Mix Cream Cheese and Cheese:
    - In a large bowl, combine the softened cream cheese and shredded cheddar cheese. Mix well until smooth and thoroughly combined.
2. Add Flavorings:
    - Stir in the chopped nuts, green onions, Worcestershire sauce, garlic powder, onion powder, paprika, salt, and black pepper. Mix until all ingredients are evenly distributed.
3. Shape the Cheese Ball:
    - Place a large piece of plastic wrap on your work surface.
    - Scoop the cheese mixture onto the plastic wrap and use your hands to shape it into a ball.
    - Wrap the cheese ball tightly with the plastic wrap and refrigerate for at least 1 hour, or until firm. This step allows the flavors to meld together.
4. Coat the Cheese Ball (Optional):
    - If desired, remove the cheese ball from the refrigerator and unwrap it.
    - Roll the cheese ball in additional chopped nuts, chopped fresh parsley, crumbled bacon bits, or everything bagel seasoning until the ball is evenly coated. This adds texture and enhances the presentation.
5. Serve:
    - Transfer the cheese ball to a serving platter.
    - Serve with your choice of crackers, pretzels, or vegetable sticks for dipping.

Tips:

- **Make-Ahead:** You can prepare the cheese ball up to 2-3 days in advance. Keep it wrapped in plastic wrap and stored in the refrigerator until ready to serve.
- **Variations:** Feel free to customize the cheese ball by adding different herbs, spices, or mix-ins like diced jalapeños or sun-dried tomatoes.
- **Presentation:** For a festive touch, shape the cheese ball into a snowman or pumpkin shape for holiday or seasonal parties.

Cheese balls are always a hit and can be easily adapted to suit your preferences. Enjoy this creamy and flavorful appetizer at your next gathering!

Deviled Eggs

Ingredients:

- 6 large eggs
- 1/4 cup mayonnaise
- 1 teaspoon Dijon mustard
- 1/2 teaspoon white vinegar or lemon juice
- Salt and pepper, to taste
- Paprika, for garnish
- Optional toppings: chopped fresh herbs (such as chives or parsley), crumbled bacon, or diced pickles

Instructions:

1. Boil the Eggs:
    - Place the eggs in a single layer in a saucepan and cover with cold water, about 1 inch above the eggs.
    - Bring the water to a boil over medium-high heat. Once boiling, cover the saucepan with a lid and remove from heat. Let the eggs sit in the hot water for 10-12 minutes for large eggs (adjust time slightly for smaller or larger eggs).
    - Drain the hot water and immediately transfer the eggs to a bowl of ice water to cool completely.
2. Prepare the Eggs:
    - Once cooled, carefully peel the eggs under cool running water to help remove the shell easily.
    - Slice each egg in half lengthwise. Gently remove the yolks and place them in a separate bowl. Arrange the egg white halves on a serving platter.
3. Make the Filling:
    - Mash the egg yolks with a fork until smooth and crumbly.
    - Add mayonnaise, Dijon mustard, white vinegar or lemon juice, salt, and pepper to the mashed yolks. Mix until well combined and creamy. Adjust the seasonings to taste.
4. Fill the Egg Whites:
    - Spoon or pipe the yolk mixture evenly into the hollows of the egg whites.
    - If desired, garnish each deviled egg with a sprinkle of paprika for color.
5. Chill and Serve:
    - Refrigerate the deviled eggs for at least 30 minutes before serving to allow the flavors to meld.
    - Serve chilled, garnished with optional toppings if desired.

Tips:

- Piping: For a more polished look, use a piping bag fitted with a star tip to fill the egg whites with the yolk mixture.
- Variations: Get creative with your deviled eggs by adding different ingredients like chopped herbs, crispy bacon, diced pickles, or a dash of hot sauce.
- Make-Ahead: You can prepare deviled eggs up to a day in advance. Keep them covered in the refrigerator until ready to serve.

Deviled eggs are a timeless appetizer that's always a crowd-pleaser at parties, potlucks, or holiday gatherings. Enjoy these creamy and flavorful treats as part of your next meal or celebration!

Pretzel Bites

Ingredients:

For the Pretzel Dough:

- 1 and 1/2 cups warm water (about 110°F)
- 1 packet (2 and 1/4 teaspoons) active dry yeast
- 1 tablespoon granulated sugar
- 4 cups all-purpose flour
- 1 teaspoon salt
- 1/4 cup unsalted butter, melted

For Boiling the Pretzel Bites:

- 10 cups water
- 2/3 cup baking soda

For Topping (optional):

- Coarse salt (such as pretzel salt)
- Melted butter for brushing

Instructions:

1. Prepare the Dough:
    - In a small bowl, combine warm water, yeast, and sugar. Let it sit for about 5 minutes until foamy.
    - In a large bowl or the bowl of a stand mixer fitted with a dough hook, combine flour and salt. Pour in the yeast mixture and melted butter. Mix on low speed until the dough comes together.
    - Knead the dough for about 5-7 minutes until smooth and elastic. If the dough is too sticky, add a bit more flour, one tablespoon at a time.
    - Place the dough in a greased bowl, cover with a clean towel or plastic wrap, and let it rise in a warm place for about 1 hour, or until doubled in size.
2. Shape the Pretzel Bites:
    - Preheat your oven to 425°F (220°C). Line a baking sheet with parchment paper or lightly grease it.
    - Punch down the risen dough to release the air. Divide the dough into smaller portions and roll each portion into ropes about 1/2 inch thick.
    - Cut the ropes into bite-sized pieces, about 1 inch in length. You can also roll each piece into a ball for a more uniform shape.
3. Boil the Pretzel Bites:
    - In a large pot, bring 10 cups of water to a boil. Carefully add the baking soda (be cautious as it may bubble up).

- Boil the pretzel bites in batches (about 10-15 at a time) for about 30 seconds, flipping them halfway through. This step gives the pretzel bites their classic chewy texture.
- Remove the pretzel bites with a slotted spoon and place them on the prepared baking sheet, making sure they are not touching each other.

4. Bake the Pretzel Bites:
   - Sprinkle the tops of the pretzel bites with coarse salt, if desired. This step is optional but adds traditional pretzel flavor.
   - Bake in the preheated oven for 12-15 minutes, or until the pretzel bites are golden brown and crisp.

5. Serve:
   - Remove from the oven and let the pretzel bites cool slightly on a wire rack.
   - If desired, brush the pretzel bites with melted butter for extra flavor.
   - Serve warm with your favorite dipping sauces, such as mustard, cheese sauce, or honey mustard.

Tips:

- **Customization:** Experiment with different toppings like cinnamon sugar, sesame seeds, or shredded cheese for varied flavors.
- **Storage:** Pretzel bites are best enjoyed fresh but can be stored in an airtight container at room temperature for up to 2 days. Reheat them in the oven for a few minutes to regain their crispiness.
- **Dipping Sauces:** Consider serving pretzel bites with a variety of dipping sauces like marinara sauce, ranch dressing, or hummus for a savory twist.

Homemade pretzel bites are a fun and delicious snack that everyone will love. Enjoy making and sharing these irresistible treats!

Chili Cheese Fries

Ingredients:

- 1 lb frozen French fries (or homemade fries if preferred)
- 1 tablespoon olive oil
- Salt and pepper, to taste

For the Chili:

- 1 lb ground beef (or ground turkey)
- 1 small onion, diced
- 2 cloves garlic, minced
- 1 can (15 oz) kidney beans, drained and rinsed
- 1 can (15 oz) diced tomatoes
- 1 can (6 oz) tomato paste
- 1 cup beef broth (or chicken broth)
- 1 tablespoon chili powder
- 1 teaspoon ground cumin
- 1/2 teaspoon paprika
- Salt and pepper, to taste

For the Cheese Sauce:

- 2 tablespoons unsalted butter
- 2 tablespoons all-purpose flour
- 1 cup milk (whole milk preferred)
- 2 cups shredded cheddar cheese
- Salt and pepper, to taste

Optional Toppings:

- Sliced jalapeños
- Chopped green onions
- Sour cream
- Guacamole or diced avocado

Instructions:

1. Prepare the French Fries:
    - Preheat your oven according to the package instructions for the frozen French fries. Toss the fries with olive oil, salt, and pepper on a baking sheet.
    - Bake the fries according to the package instructions until they are crispy and golden brown.
2. Make the Chili:

- In a large skillet or pot, cook the ground beef over medium-high heat until browned and cooked through, breaking it up with a spoon as it cooks.
- Add the diced onion and garlic to the skillet with the cooked beef. Cook for 2-3 minutes until the onion is softened.
- Stir in the kidney beans, diced tomatoes, tomato paste, beef broth, chili powder, cumin, paprika, salt, and pepper. Bring the mixture to a simmer.
- Reduce the heat to low and let the chili simmer for 15-20 minutes, stirring occasionally, until thickened. Taste and adjust seasoning as needed.

3. Make the Cheese Sauce:
   - In a medium saucepan, melt the butter over medium heat. Whisk in the flour and cook for 1-2 minutes until smooth and bubbling.
   - Gradually whisk in the milk, stirring constantly until the mixture is smooth and thickened.
   - Reduce the heat to low and stir in the shredded cheddar cheese until melted and smooth. Season with salt and pepper to taste.
4. Assemble Chili Cheese Fries:
   - Arrange the crispy fries on a serving platter or individual plates.
   - Spoon the warm chili over the fries, followed by the cheese sauce.
   - If desired, top with sliced jalapeños, chopped green onions, sour cream, guacamole, or diced avocado.
5. Serve Immediately:
   - Serve the chili cheese fries immediately while hot and enjoy!

Tips:

- **Homemade Fries:** For homemade fries, peel and cut potatoes into thin strips. Soak in cold water for 30 minutes, then pat dry. Toss with olive oil, salt, and pepper, and bake until crispy.
- **Make-Ahead:** Prepare the chili and cheese sauce ahead of time and store them in separate airtight containers in the refrigerator. Reheat gently before assembling the chili cheese fries.
- **Variations:** Customize your chili cheese fries by using different types of cheese, adding bacon bits, or using sweet potato fries for a healthier twist.

Chili cheese fries are a hearty and satisfying dish that's perfect for game days, parties, or as a comforting meal. Enjoy this delicious combination of flavors and textures!

Mozzarella Sticks

Ingredients:

- 12 mozzarella string cheese sticks
- 1 cup all-purpose flour
- 2 large eggs, beaten
- 1 cup Italian-style breadcrumbs (or plain breadcrumbs seasoned with Italian seasoning)
- 1/2 cup grated Parmesan cheese
- 1/2 teaspoon garlic powder
- 1/2 teaspoon onion powder
- 1/2 teaspoon dried oregano
- 1/2 teaspoon dried basil
- Salt and pepper, to taste
- Vegetable oil, for frying
- Marinara sauce, for dipping

Instructions:

1. Prepare the Mozzarella Sticks:
    - Cut each mozzarella stick in half to make 24 shorter sticks. Place them on a baking sheet lined with parchment paper and freeze for about 30 minutes to firm up.
2. Set Up the Breading Station:
    - In one shallow bowl or plate, place the flour. In another shallow bowl, beat the eggs. In a third bowl, combine the breadcrumbs, grated Parmesan cheese, garlic powder, onion powder, dried oregano, dried basil, salt, and pepper.
3. Bread the Mozzarella Sticks:
    - Working in batches, coat each frozen mozzarella stick first in the flour (shake off excess), then dip in the beaten eggs, and finally coat thoroughly in the breadcrumb mixture. Press gently to adhere the breadcrumbs.
    - Place the breaded mozzarella sticks back on the baking sheet. Freeze again for about 15-20 minutes to set the breading.
4. Fry the Mozzarella Sticks:
    - In a large, deep skillet or Dutch oven, heat about 2 inches of vegetable oil over medium-high heat until it reaches 350°F (175°C).
    - Carefully add a few mozzarella sticks to the hot oil, being careful not to overcrowd the pan. Fry for about 1-2 minutes, turning occasionally, until golden brown and crispy.
    - Remove the fried mozzarella sticks with a slotted spoon and transfer them to a plate lined with paper towels to drain excess oil. Repeat with the remaining mozzarella sticks.
5. Serve:

- Arrange the hot mozzarella sticks on a serving platter and serve immediately with marinara sauce for dipping.

Tips:

- **Breading Tips:** Double coating the mozzarella sticks (flour, egg, breadcrumbs) ensures a crispier exterior.
- **Freezing:** Freezing the mozzarella sticks before and after breading helps them maintain their shape and prevents the cheese from melting too quickly during frying.
- **Baking Option:** For a healthier alternative, you can bake the breaded mozzarella sticks in a preheated oven at 400°F (200°C) for about 8-10 minutes until golden brown and crispy.

Homemade mozzarella sticks are a crowd-pleasing appetizer that's perfect for parties, game days, or anytime you're craving a cheesy snack. Enjoy the crispy exterior and melty cheese center with your favorite dipping sauce!

Potato Skins

Ingredients:

- 4 large russet potatoes, scrubbed clean
- 2 tablespoons olive oil
- Salt and pepper, to taste
- 1 cup shredded cheddar cheese (or cheese of your choice)
- 4 slices cooked bacon, crumbled
- 2 green onions, thinly sliced
- Sour cream, for serving
- Optional: chopped fresh parsley or cilantro for garnish

Instructions:

1. Prepare the Potatoes:
   - Preheat your oven to 400°F (200°C).
   - Pierce each potato several times with a fork or knife to allow steam to escape during baking.
   - Rub the potatoes with olive oil and season generously with salt and pepper.
2. Bake the Potatoes:
   - Place the potatoes directly on the oven rack or on a baking sheet lined with foil.
   - Bake for 45-60 minutes, or until the potatoes are tender when pierced with a fork.
3. Prepare the Potato Skins:
   - Remove the potatoes from the oven and let them cool slightly until they are safe to handle.
   - Cut each potato in half lengthwise. Carefully scoop out most of the flesh, leaving about 1/4 inch thickness of potato attached to the skin.
4. Bake the Potato Skins:
   - Increase the oven temperature to 450°F (230°C).
   - Place the hollowed-out potato skins on a baking sheet, skin side down.
   - Brush the insides of the potato skins with a bit more olive oil and season with additional salt and pepper if desired.
   - Bake for about 10 minutes, or until the edges are crispy and lightly browned.
5. Add Toppings:
   - Remove the potato skins from the oven and sprinkle each with shredded cheddar cheese and crumbled bacon.
6. Return to Oven:
   - Return the potato skins to the oven and bake for another 2-3 minutes, or until the cheese is melted and bubbly.
7. Serve:
   - Remove the potato skins from the oven and let them cool for a minute or two.
   - Garnish with sliced green onions and a dollop of sour cream.
   - Optionally, sprinkle with chopped fresh parsley or cilantro for added freshness.

8. Enjoy:
   - Serve the potato skins warm as a delicious appetizer or snack.

Tips:

- Variations: Feel free to customize your potato skins with different toppings such as diced tomatoes, jalapeños, or even shredded chicken for a heartier version.
- Make-Ahead: You can bake the potatoes and prepare the potato skins (step 3) ahead of time. Store the cooled potato skins in an airtight container in the refrigerator for up to 2 days. When ready to serve, simply add the toppings and bake as directed.
- Using Leftover Potato Flesh: Don't discard the scooped-out potato flesh! Use it in other recipes like mashed potatoes, potato soup, or potato pancakes.

Homemade potato skins are a crowd-pleasing dish that's perfect for parties, game days, or as a comforting snack. Enjoy the crispy texture of the potato skins paired with the cheesy, bacony goodness inside!

Onion Rings

Ingredients:

- 2 large onions (yellow or sweet onions)
- 1 cup all-purpose flour
- 1 teaspoon baking powder
- 1/2 teaspoon salt
- 1/4 teaspoon black pepper
- 1 cup cold sparkling water (or beer)
- Vegetable oil, for frying

Instructions:

1. Prepare the Onions:
    - Peel the onions and cut them into slices about 1/2-inch thick. Separate the slices into individual rings.
2. Prepare the Batter:
    - In a large bowl, whisk together the flour, baking powder, salt, and black pepper.
    - Gradually pour in the cold sparkling water (or beer), whisking continuously until the batter is smooth and free of lumps. The batter should be thick enough to coat the onion rings but still pourable.
3. Heat the Oil:
    - Pour enough vegetable oil into a deep fryer or large, heavy-bottomed pot to reach a depth of about 2 inches. Heat the oil to 375°F (190°C).
4. Coat the Onion Rings:
    - Working in batches, dip the onion rings into the batter, making sure each ring is well coated.
5. Fry the Onion Rings:
    - Carefully place the battered onion rings into the hot oil, a few at a time, making sure not to overcrowd the pot. Fry for about 2-3 minutes, flipping halfway through, until golden brown and crispy.
6. Drain and Serve:
    - Remove the fried onion rings with a slotted spoon or tongs and transfer them to a plate lined with paper towels to drain excess oil.
7. Season and Enjoy:
    - Season the hot onion rings with a pinch of salt while they are still warm.
    - Serve immediately with your favorite dipping sauce, such as ketchup, ranch dressing, or spicy mayo.

Tips:

- Uniformity: Try to cut the onions into rings of similar thickness to ensure even cooking.

- Batter Consistency: Adjust the amount of sparkling water (or beer) to achieve the desired consistency of the batter—thick enough to coat the onions but not too thick.
- Keep Warm: If making large batches, keep the fried onion rings warm in a low oven (around 200°F or 90°C) on a baking sheet lined with a wire rack while frying subsequent batches.

Homemade onion rings are a delightful treat that's sure to be a hit at any gathering or meal. Enjoy the crispy exterior and tender, sweet onion inside for a delicious snack or side dish!

Pizza Rolls

Ingredients:

- 1 lb pizza dough (store-bought or homemade)
- 1/2 cup pizza sauce
- 1 cup shredded mozzarella cheese
- 1/2 cup finely chopped pepperoni (or other toppings like cooked sausage, bell peppers, mushrooms, etc.)
- 1 tablespoon olive oil
- 1/2 teaspoon garlic powder
- 1/2 teaspoon dried oregano
- Marinara sauce, for dipping (optional)

Instructions:

1. Prepare the Pizza Dough:
    - If using store-bought pizza dough, follow the package instructions for bringing it to room temperature. If making homemade dough, prepare it according to your favorite recipe.
2. Preheat the Oven:
    - Preheat your oven to 425°F (220°C). Line a baking sheet with parchment paper.
3. Roll Out the Dough:
    - On a lightly floured surface, roll out the pizza dough into a rectangle about 1/4 inch thick.
4. Assemble the Pizza Rolls:
    - Spread the pizza sauce evenly over the rolled-out dough, leaving a small border around the edges.
    - Sprinkle the shredded mozzarella cheese over the sauce, followed by the chopped pepperoni (or other toppings).
5. Roll Up the Dough:
    - Starting from one long side, tightly roll up the dough into a log shape.
6. Slice into Rolls:
    - Using a sharp knife, slice the rolled-up dough into 1-inch thick slices. You should get about 12-15 pizza rolls depending on the size of your log.
7. Arrange on Baking Sheet:
    - Place the pizza rolls on the prepared baking sheet, with the cut sides facing up.
8. Season and Bake:
    - In a small bowl, mix together the olive oil, garlic powder, and dried oregano. Brush the mixture over the tops of the pizza rolls.
    - Bake in the preheated oven for 15-18 minutes, or until the rolls are golden brown and the cheese is melted and bubbly.
9. Serve:
    - Remove from the oven and let the pizza rolls cool slightly before serving.

- Optionally, serve with marinara sauce for dipping.

Tips:

- **Variations:** Feel free to customize your pizza rolls with different toppings such as cooked sausage, diced bell peppers, mushrooms, or even a mix of cheeses.
- **Make-Ahead:** You can assemble the pizza rolls up to a day in advance. Cover them tightly with plastic wrap and refrigerate until ready to bake. Bake as directed when ready to serve.
- **Freezing:** If you want to freeze pizza rolls, place the unbaked rolls on a baking sheet and freeze until solid. Transfer to a freezer bag or container for long-term storage. Bake from frozen, adding a few extra minutes to the baking time.

Homemade pizza rolls are a fun and delicious snack or appetizer that's sure to be a hit with both kids and adults. Enjoy the flavors of pizza in a convenient and bite-sized form!

Garlic Knots

Ingredients:

For the Dough:

- 3 cups all-purpose flour
- 1 teaspoon salt
- 1 tablespoon granulated sugar
- 2 and 1/4 teaspoons (1 packet) active dry yeast
- 1 cup warm water (about 110°F)
- 2 tablespoons olive oil

For the Garlic Butter:

- 1/2 cup unsalted butter, melted
- 3-4 cloves garlic, minced (adjust to taste)
- 2 tablespoons chopped fresh parsley (or 1 tablespoon dried parsley)
- 1/4 teaspoon salt

For Finishing:

- Grated Parmesan cheese, for sprinkling (optional)
- Additional chopped parsley, for garnish (optional)

Instructions:

1. Prepare the Dough:
    - In a large mixing bowl or the bowl of a stand mixer fitted with a dough hook, combine the warm water, sugar, and yeast. Let it sit for about 5-10 minutes until foamy.
    - Add the flour and salt to the yeast mixture. Mix on low speed until the dough comes together.
    - Add the olive oil and knead the dough for about 5-7 minutes until smooth and elastic. If the dough is too sticky, add a little more flour, one tablespoon at a time.
    - Place the dough in a lightly greased bowl, cover with a clean kitchen towel or plastic wrap, and let it rise in a warm place for about 1 hour or until doubled in size.
2. Shape the Garlic Knots:
    - Preheat your oven to 400°F (200°C). Line a baking sheet with parchment paper.
    - Punch down the risen dough to release the air. Divide the dough into 16 equal pieces.
    - Roll each piece of dough into a rope about 8 inches long. Tie each rope into a knot and tuck the ends underneath. Place the knots on the prepared baking sheet, leaving space between each knot.

3. Bake the Garlic Knots:
   - Bake in the preheated oven for 12-15 minutes, or until the knots are golden brown.
4. Prepare the Garlic Butter:
   - While the knots are baking, prepare the garlic butter. In a small saucepan or microwave-safe bowl, melt the butter.
   - Stir in the minced garlic, chopped parsley, and salt into the melted butter.
5. Coat the Garlic Knots:
   - Remove the knots from the oven and immediately brush them generously with the garlic butter mixture while they are still hot.
6. Serve:
   - Sprinkle the warm garlic knots with grated Parmesan cheese and additional chopped parsley if desired.
   - Serve the garlic knots warm as a delicious appetizer or side dish.

Tips:

- Variations: For a cheesy twist, sprinkle grated mozzarella or Parmesan cheese on top of the knots before baking.
- Make-Ahead: Garlic knots are best enjoyed fresh, but you can freeze them after baking. Reheat in the oven for a few minutes before serving.
- Dipping Sauces: Serve garlic knots with marinara sauce, pesto, or creamy garlic dipping sauce for extra flavor.

Homemade garlic knots are a flavorful and comforting addition to any meal. Enjoy the soft, fluffy texture combined with the savory garlic butter and herbs—it's sure to be a hit with family and friends!

Shrimp Cocktail

Ingredients:

For the Shrimp:

- 1 lb large shrimp, peeled and deveined (tails on or off, as desired)
- Salt and pepper, to taste
- 1 lemon, halved

For the Cocktail Sauce:

- 1/2 cup ketchup
- 2 tablespoons prepared horseradish (adjust to taste)
- 1 tablespoon lemon juice
- 1 teaspoon Worcestershire sauce
- 1/2 teaspoon hot sauce (optional)
- Salt and pepper, to taste

For Serving:

- Fresh parsley, for garnish
- Lemon wedges, for serving

Instructions:

1. Prepare the Shrimp:
    - Fill a large pot with water and add a generous pinch of salt. Squeeze in the juice from one half of the lemon and add the lemon half to the water.
    - Bring the water to a boil over high heat. Add the shrimp and cook for 2-3 minutes, or until the shrimp are pink and opaque. Be careful not to overcook them.
    - Drain the shrimp and immediately transfer them to a bowl of ice water to stop the cooking process and cool them down quickly. Once cooled, drain again and pat dry with paper towels.
2. Prepare the Cocktail Sauce:
    - In a small bowl, combine the ketchup, prepared horseradish, lemon juice, Worcestershire sauce, hot sauce (if using), salt, and pepper. Adjust the seasoning and horseradish to taste. Stir well to combine.
3. Chill:
    - Transfer the cocktail sauce to a serving bowl and refrigerate until ready to serve.
4. Serve:
    - Arrange the chilled shrimp on a serving platter or individual cocktail glasses.
    - Garnish with fresh parsley and lemon wedges.
    - Serve the shrimp cocktail with the chilled cocktail sauce on the side.

Tips:

- Choosing Shrimp: Use fresh or thawed frozen shrimp for the best results. Look for shrimp that are firm, pink, and have a mild odor.
- Cooking Shrimp: Be careful not to overcook the shrimp as they can become rubbery. The shrimp should turn opaque and curl into a C shape when cooked properly.
- Make-Ahead: You can cook the shrimp and prepare the cocktail sauce ahead of time. Keep the shrimp refrigerated until ready to serve.

Shrimp cocktail is a refreshing and elegant appetizer that's perfect for parties, special occasions, or as a starter before a meal. Enjoy the combination of tender shrimp with the zesty cocktail sauce for a delicious culinary experience!

Chicken Taquitos

Ingredients:

- 2 cups shredded cooked chicken (rotisserie chicken works well)
- 1 cup shredded Monterey Jack or cheddar cheese
- 1/2 cup salsa (choose your preferred level of spiciness)
- 1/2 teaspoon ground cumin
- 1/2 teaspoon chili powder
- 1/4 teaspoon garlic powder
- 1/4 teaspoon onion powder
- Salt and pepper, to taste
- 12-15 small corn or flour tortillas
- Vegetable oil, for frying
- Sour cream, guacamole, or salsa, for serving (optional)
- Chopped fresh cilantro, for garnish (optional)
- Lime wedges, for serving (optional)

Instructions:

1. Prepare the Filling:
    - In a mixing bowl, combine the shredded chicken, shredded cheese, salsa, ground cumin, chili powder, garlic powder, onion powder, salt, and pepper. Mix well until evenly combined.
2. Assemble the Taquitos:
    - Warm the tortillas in the microwave for a few seconds or until they are pliable. This makes them easier to roll.
    - Place about 2 tablespoons of the chicken filling along one edge of each tortilla.
    - Roll up the tortilla tightly around the filling to form a taquito. Secure the edge with a toothpick if needed to keep it closed.
3. Fry the Taquitos:
    - In a large skillet or frying pan, heat about 1/2 inch of vegetable oil over medium-high heat until hot but not smoking.
    - Carefully place a few taquitos seam-side down in the hot oil, making sure not to overcrowd the pan.
    - Fry the taquitos for 2-3 minutes per side, or until they are golden brown and crispy all over. Use tongs to gently turn them to cook evenly.
    - Once cooked, transfer the taquitos to a plate lined with paper towels to drain excess oil. Remove any toothpicks.
4. Serve:
    - Serve the chicken taquitos warm with sour cream, guacamole, salsa, or your favorite dipping sauce on the side.
    - Garnish with chopped fresh cilantro and serve with lime wedges for squeezing over the taquitos.

Tips:

- Baking Option: If you prefer a healthier alternative, you can bake the taquitos instead of frying them. Preheat your oven to 400°F (200°C) and place the rolled taquitos seam-side down on a baking sheet lined with parchment paper. Lightly brush or spray them with oil. Bake for 15-20 minutes, or until crispy and golden brown.
- Freezing: You can freeze uncooked taquitos for later. Arrange the rolled taquitos on a baking sheet and freeze until solid, then transfer them to a freezer bag or container. Fry or bake them from frozen, adding a few extra minutes to the cooking time.
- Variations: Feel free to customize the filling by adding diced green chilies, black beans, corn, or any other favorite ingredients.

Homemade chicken taquitos are a delicious appetizer or main dish that's perfect for parties, game days, or family dinners. Enjoy the crispy texture and flavorful filling of these Mexican-inspired delights!

Salsa

Ingredients:

- 4 large tomatoes, diced
- 1/2 onion, finely chopped
- 1 jalapeño or serrano pepper, seeded and minced (adjust to taste)
- 2 cloves garlic, minced
- 1/4 cup chopped fresh cilantro
- 2 tablespoons fresh lime juice (about 1 lime)
- 1/2 teaspoon ground cumin
- Salt and pepper, to taste

Optional Additions for Variation:

- 1/2 bell pepper, diced (for added crunch and sweetness)
- 1/2 teaspoon chili powder (for extra heat)
- 1/2 teaspoon sugar (to balance acidity)
- Diced mango, pineapple, or avocado (for a fruity twist)

Instructions:

1. Prepare the Ingredients:
   - Dice the tomatoes, finely chop the onion, mince the garlic, and seed and mince the jalapeño or serrano pepper.
2. Combine Ingredients:
   - In a mixing bowl, combine the diced tomatoes, chopped onion, minced jalapeño or serrano pepper, minced garlic, and chopped cilantro.
3. Season the Salsa:
   - Add the fresh lime juice, ground cumin, salt, and pepper to taste. Adjust the seasonings according to your preference.
4. Mix Well:
   - Gently stir all the ingredients together until well combined. Taste and adjust seasoning if necessary.
5. Chill (Optional):
   - For best flavor, let the salsa sit in the refrigerator for at least 30 minutes to allow the flavors to meld together.
6. Serve:
   - Serve the salsa fresh as a dip with tortilla chips, or use it as a topping for tacos, burritos, grilled meats, or fish.

Tips:

- Customization: Salsa is highly customizable. Feel free to adjust the ingredients and quantities to suit your taste preferences. For example, you can add more chili for spiciness, or more lime juice for tanginess.
- Texture: If you prefer a smoother salsa, you can pulse the ingredients in a food processor briefly. For a chunkier salsa, simply chop ingredients finely.
- Storage: Store leftover salsa in an airtight container in the refrigerator for up to 5 days. Stir well before serving.

This basic salsa recipe is a great starting point, and you can experiment with different ingredients and levels of spiciness to create your perfect salsa. Enjoy the fresh and vibrant flavors of homemade salsa with your favorite dishes!

Spinach Dip

Ingredients:

- 8 oz (about 225g) cream cheese, softened
- 1/2 cup sour cream
- 1/2 cup mayonnaise
- 1 cup shredded mozzarella cheese (or a mix of mozzarella and Parmesan)
- 1/2 cup grated Parmesan cheese
- 1 clove garlic, minced
- 1/2 teaspoon onion powder
- 1/4 teaspoon black pepper
- 1/4 teaspoon salt
- 10 oz (about 300g) frozen chopped spinach, thawed and well-drained
- 1/2 cup chopped water chestnuts (optional, for crunch)
- 1/4 cup chopped green onions (optional, for garnish)

Instructions:

1. Prepare the Spinach:
   - Thaw the frozen spinach according to package instructions. Once thawed, squeeze out excess moisture using a clean kitchen towel or paper towels. Ensure the spinach is well-drained to prevent the dip from becoming watery.
2. Mix the Dip:
   - In a large mixing bowl, combine the softened cream cheese, sour cream, mayonnaise, shredded mozzarella cheese, grated Parmesan cheese, minced garlic, onion powder, black pepper, and salt. Mix until well combined and smooth.
3. Add Spinach and Optional Ingredients:
   - Stir in the well-drained chopped spinach and chopped water chestnuts (if using) until evenly distributed throughout the dip.
4. Chill (Optional):
   - For best flavor, cover the bowl and refrigerate the spinach dip for at least 1 hour before serving. This allows the flavors to meld together.
5. Serve:
   - Garnish the spinach dip with chopped green onions if desired.
   - Serve the spinach dip with your choice of dippers such as tortilla chips, sliced baguette, crackers, or fresh vegetable sticks.

Tips:

- Variations: Add diced artichoke hearts for a spinach and artichoke dip variation, or sprinkle with crispy bacon bits for added flavor.
- Make-Ahead: You can prepare the spinach dip a day in advance. Store it covered in the refrigerator until ready to serve.

- Warm Spinach Dip: If you prefer a warm spinach dip, transfer the mixed dip to an oven-safe dish and bake at 350°F (175°C) for about 20-25 minutes, or until heated through and bubbly.

Spinach dip is a crowd-pleasing appetizer that's creamy, savory, and packed with flavor. Enjoy this classic dip at your next gathering or as a tasty snack!

Ham and Cheese Sliders

Ingredients:

- 12 slider rolls or dinner rolls
- 12 slices of deli ham
- 12 slices of Swiss cheese (or your favorite cheese)
- 1/2 cup unsalted butter, melted
- 1 tablespoon Dijon mustard
- 1 tablespoon Worcestershire sauce
- 1 tablespoon poppy seeds (optional)
- 1 tablespoon dried minced onion (optional)
- 1/2 teaspoon garlic powder
- Salt and pepper, to taste
- Fresh parsley or green onions, chopped (for garnish, optional)

Instructions:

1. Preheat the Oven:
    - Preheat your oven to 350°F (175°C). Grease a baking dish or line it with parchment paper.
2. Prepare the Sliders:
    - Slice the slider rolls in half horizontally and place the bottom halves in the prepared baking dish.
3. Layer Ham and Cheese:
    - Layer each slider roll bottom with a slice of ham and a slice of Swiss cheese. You can fold the ham slices to fit the rolls.
4. Assemble Sliders:
    - Place the top halves of the slider rolls over the ham and cheese to close each sandwich.
5. Make the Butter Sauce:
    - In a small bowl, whisk together the melted butter, Dijon mustard, Worcestershire sauce, poppy seeds (if using), dried minced onion (if using), garlic powder, salt, and pepper.
6. Brush Sliders:
    - Brush the butter sauce generously over the tops of the slider rolls, making sure to coat each one evenly.
7. Bake:
    - Cover the baking dish with aluminum foil and bake in the preheated oven for 10-15 minutes, or until the cheese is melted and the sliders are heated through.
8. Optional: Toast Tops (Broil):
    - If desired, uncover the sliders and broil them for an additional 1-2 minutes, or until the tops are lightly toasted and golden brown.
9. Serve:

- Remove from the oven and let the sliders cool slightly before serving.
- Garnish with chopped fresh parsley or green onions if desired.

Tips:

- **Variations:** Feel free to customize your sliders by using different types of cheese (like cheddar or provolone) or adding sliced pickles, mustard, or mayo before assembling.
- **Make-Ahead:** You can assemble the sliders ahead of time and refrigerate them covered in foil. Bake them when ready to serve.
- **Serving:** Serve these sliders warm as a snack, appetizer, or main dish alongside a salad or soup.

Ham and cheese sliders are a crowd-pleasing dish that's simple to prepare and packed with flavor. Whether for a party or a quick meal, these sliders are sure to be a hit!

Beef Empanadas

Ingredients:

For the Dough:

- 2 cups all-purpose flour
- 1/2 teaspoon salt
- 1/2 cup unsalted butter, cold and cut into cubes
- 1 egg
- 1/3 cup cold water
- 1 tablespoon white vinegar

For the Filling:

- 1 tablespoon olive oil
- 1 small onion, finely chopped
- 2 cloves garlic, minced
- 1/2 lb ground beef
- 1/2 teaspoon ground cumin
- 1/2 teaspoon paprika
- Salt and pepper to taste
- 1/4 cup chopped green olives (optional)
- 2 hard-boiled eggs, chopped (optional)

For Assembly:

- 1 egg, beaten (for egg wash)

Instructions:

1. Prepare the Dough:

   1. In a large bowl, whisk together the flour and salt.
   2. Add the cold butter cubes and use your fingers or a pastry cutter to cut the butter into the flour until the mixture resembles coarse crumbs.
   3. In a separate small bowl, whisk together the egg, water, and vinegar.
   4. Gradually add the egg mixture to the flour mixture, stirring until the dough just starts to come together.
   5. Turn the dough out onto a clean surface and knead briefly until smooth. Wrap in plastic wrap and refrigerate for at least 30 minutes.

2. Make the Filling:

   1. Heat olive oil in a skillet over medium heat. Add onions and cook until softened, about 3-4 minutes.

2. Add minced garlic and cook for another 1-2 minutes until fragrant.
3. Add ground beef to the skillet, breaking it up with a spoon. Cook until browned and cooked through.
4. Stir in cumin, paprika, salt, and pepper. Add chopped olives and hard-boiled eggs if using. Remove from heat and let cool.

3. Assemble the Empanadas:

1. Preheat oven to 375°F (190°C). Line a baking sheet with parchment paper.
2. On a lightly floured surface, roll out the chilled dough to about 1/8 inch thickness. Using a round cutter or a small bowl, cut out circles of dough (approximately 4-5 inches in diameter).
3. Place a spoonful of the beef filling in the center of each dough circle.
4. Fold the dough over the filling to create a half-moon shape. Press the edges together with your fingers or a fork to seal.
5. Place the assembled empanadas on the prepared baking sheet. Brush the tops with beaten egg for a golden finish.
6. Bake for 20-25 minutes, or until golden brown and crispy.

4. Serve:

1. Allow the empanadas to cool slightly before serving. They can be enjoyed warm or at room temperature.
2. Serve with chimichurri sauce or your favorite dipping sauce.

Enjoy your homemade beef empanadas! They are perfect as appetizers, snacks, or even a main course served with a side salad.

Sweet and Spicy Nuts

Ingredients:

- 2 cups mixed nuts (such as almonds, cashews, pecans, walnuts)
- 1/4 cup brown sugar
- 1/4 cup granulated sugar
- 1 teaspoon salt
- 1 teaspoon ground cinnamon
- 1/2 teaspoon ground cayenne pepper (adjust to taste for spiciness)
- 1/4 cup water
- 1 tablespoon butter
- 1 teaspoon vanilla extract

Instructions:

1. Preheat Oven:

- Preheat your oven to 350°F (175°C). Line a baking sheet with parchment paper or a silicone baking mat.

2. Prepare the Sugar Coating:

   1. In a small bowl, mix together the brown sugar, granulated sugar, salt, cinnamon, and cayenne pepper. Set aside.

3. Cook the Syrup:

   1. In a medium saucepan, combine the water, butter, and vanilla extract. Heat over medium-high heat until the butter is melted and the mixture begins to simmer.

4. Coat the Nuts.

   1. Add the mixed nuts to the saucepan with the butter mixture. Stir to coat the nuts evenly.
   2. Cook the nuts in the syrup for about 2-3 minutes, stirring constantly, until the syrup thickens slightly and coats the nuts.

5. Bake the Nuts:

   1. Spread the coated nuts in a single layer on the prepared baking sheet.
   2. Bake in the preheated oven for 15-20 minutes, stirring once halfway through baking, until the nuts are golden brown and caramelized.

6. Cool and Serve:

1. Remove the baking sheet from the oven and let the nuts cool completely on the baking sheet. They will become crunchy as they cool.
2. Once cooled, break apart any clusters of nuts.

7. Enjoy:

1. Serve the sweet and spicy nuts as a snack or appetizer. They can be stored in an airtight container at room temperature for up to two weeks.

These sweet and spicy nuts are perfect for parties, movie nights, or as a tasty homemade gift. Adjust the level of spiciness according to your preference, and enjoy the addictive combination of sweet, spicy, and crunchy flavors!

Popcorn

Ingredients:

- 1/2 cup popcorn kernels
- 2-3 tablespoons vegetable oil or coconut oil
- Salt, to taste
- Optional toppings: melted butter, grated cheese, nutritional yeast, cinnamon sugar, etc.

Instructions:

1. Heat the Oil:

   1. In a large, heavy-bottomed pot with a lid, heat the oil over medium-high heat. Use enough oil to coat the bottom of the pot and allow the kernels to move freely.

2. Add Popcorn Kernels:

   1. Once the oil is hot (test by adding a few kernels; they should sizzle), add the popcorn kernels in an even layer.

3. Cover and Shake:

   1. Cover the pot with the lid. As the kernels begin to pop, shake the pot gently back and forth to ensure even popping and to prevent burning.

4. Continue Popping:

   1. Keep shaking the pot intermittently until the popping sound slows down to 2-3 seconds between pops. This indicates that most of the kernels have popped.

5. Seasoning:

   1. Remove the pot from heat and immediately transfer the popcorn to a large bowl.
   2. Season with salt and any additional toppings or seasonings of your choice. Toss well to coat evenly.

6. Serve:

   1. Enjoy your freshly made stovetop popcorn as a snack or with your favorite movie or TV show!

Tips for Perfect Popcorn:

- Even Heating: Ensure the oil is evenly distributed and the kernels are in a single layer to prevent uneven popping.

- Shaking Technique: Shake the pot gently but frequently to avoid burning and to encourage even popping.
- Toppings: Get creative with toppings! Melted butter, nutritional yeast, grated cheese, chili powder, or even a drizzle of caramel or chocolate can add a unique twist to your popcorn.

Stovetop popcorn is a healthier alternative to microwave popcorn and allows for customization to suit your taste preferences. It's a great snack that's quick to make and perfect for any occasion!

Stuffed Peppers

Ingredients:

- 4 large bell peppers (any color)
- 1 tablespoon olive oil
- 1 onion, diced
- 2 cloves garlic, minced
- 1 lb ground beef (or turkey/chicken)
- 1 cup cooked rice (white or brown)
- 1 can (14 oz) diced tomatoes, drained
- 1 teaspoon dried oregano
- 1 teaspoon dried basil
- Salt and pepper, to taste
- 1 cup shredded cheese (cheddar, mozzarella, or your choice)
- Chopped fresh parsley, for garnish (optional)

Instructions:

1. Preheat the Oven:

    1. Preheat your oven to 375°F (190°C). Lightly grease a baking dish large enough to hold the peppers upright.

2. Prepare the Peppers:

    1. Cut the tops off the bell peppers and remove the seeds and membranes from inside. Rinse them under cold water.

3. Cook the Filling:

    1. Heat olive oil in a large skillet over medium heat. Add the diced onion and cook until softened, about 5 minutes.
    2. Add minced garlic and cook for 1 minute until fragrant.
    3. Add the ground beef to the skillet, breaking it up with a spoon. Cook until browned and cooked through.
    4. Stir in the cooked rice, diced tomatoes, dried oregano, dried basil, salt, and pepper. Cook for another 2-3 minutes until heated through. Taste and adjust seasoning if needed.

4. Stuff the Peppers:

    1. Spoon the beef and rice mixture evenly into the hollowed-out bell peppers, pressing down gently to pack the filling.

5. Bake the Stuffed Peppers:

1. Place the stuffed peppers upright in the prepared baking dish. Cover the dish loosely with foil.
2. Bake in the preheated oven for 30-35 minutes, or until the peppers are tender.

6. Add Cheese and Finish Baking:

    1. Remove the foil from the baking dish. Sprinkle the shredded cheese evenly over the tops of the stuffed peppers.
    2. Return the peppers to the oven and bake, uncovered, for an additional 10 minutes or until the cheese is melted and bubbly.

7. Serve:

    1. Remove the stuffed peppers from the oven and let them cool slightly before serving.
    2. Garnish with chopped fresh parsley if desired.

Enjoy your delicious stuffed peppers as a satisfying main dish! They pair well with a side salad or garlic bread for a complete meal.

Chicken Tenders

Ingredients:

- 1 lb chicken tenders (or boneless, skinless chicken breasts cut into strips)
- 1 cup all-purpose flour
- 1 teaspoon salt
- 1/2 teaspoon black pepper
- 1/2 teaspoon paprika
- 1/2 teaspoon garlic powder
- 2 eggs
- 2 tablespoons milk or buttermilk
- 1 cup breadcrumbs (plain or seasoned)
- Cooking oil (such as vegetable oil or canola oil), for frying

Optional Dipping Sauces:

- Honey mustard
- BBQ sauce
- Ranch dressing
- Buffalo sauce

Instructions:

1. Prepare the Chicken:

    1. If using chicken breasts, cut them into strips about 1 inch wide.
    2. Pat the chicken tenders dry with paper towels to remove any excess moisture.

2. Set Up Dredging Stations:

    1. In a shallow dish, combine the flour, salt, pepper, paprika, and garlic powder.
    2. In another shallow dish, whisk together the eggs and milk (or buttermilk).
    3. Place the breadcrumbs in a third shallow dish.

3. Dredge the Chicken:

    1. Dredge each chicken tender in the seasoned flour mixture, shaking off any excess.
    2. Dip the floured chicken tender into the egg mixture, coating evenly.
    3. Finally, coat the chicken tender with breadcrumbs, pressing gently to adhere. Place on a plate or baking sheet.

4. Fry the Chicken Tenders:

1. In a large skillet or frying pan, heat about 1/2 inch of cooking oil over medium-high heat until hot (around 350°F or 175°C).
2. Carefully place the breaded chicken tenders in the hot oil, making sure not to overcrowd the pan. You may need to fry in batches.
3. Fry the chicken tenders for about 3-4 minutes per side, or until golden brown and cooked through. The internal temperature should reach 165°F (74°C).
4. Remove the cooked chicken tenders from the oil and place them on a plate lined with paper towels to drain excess oil.

5. Serve:

1. Serve the crispy chicken tenders hot with your favorite dipping sauces.
2. Enjoy as a snack, appetizer, or main course with sides like French fries, coleslaw, or a salad.

Tips for Crispy Chicken Tenders:

- Oil Temperature: Maintain a consistent oil temperature to ensure crispy chicken tenders without them absorbing too much oil.
- Breadcrumbs: Use plain or seasoned breadcrumbs according to your preference. Panko breadcrumbs can also be used for extra crunch.
- Oven Baking Option: For a healthier alternative, you can bake the breaded chicken tenders in a preheated oven at 400°F (200°C) for about 15-20 minutes, turning halfway through, until golden brown and cooked through.

Homemade chicken tenders are a crowd-pleasing dish that's sure to be a hit with both kids and adults alike!

Mac and Cheese Bites

Ingredients:

- 2 cups cooked macaroni pasta
- 1 1/2 cups shredded cheddar cheese (or your favorite cheese blend)
- 1/2 cup grated Parmesan cheese
- 1/2 cup milk
- 1/4 cup unsalted butter
- 1 tablespoon all-purpose flour
- 1/2 teaspoon salt
- 1/4 teaspoon black pepper
- 1/4 teaspoon paprika (optional)
- 1/4 teaspoon garlic powder (optional)
- 2 eggs, beaten
- 1 cup seasoned breadcrumbs
- Cooking spray or oil, for greasing

Instructions:

1. Prepare the Macaroni and Cheese:

    1. Cook the macaroni pasta according to package instructions until al dente. Drain and set aside.
    2. In a large saucepan, melt the butter over medium heat. Stir in the flour and cook for about 1 minute, stirring constantly, to make a roux.
    3. Gradually whisk in the milk until smooth and thickened, about 3-4 minutes.
    4. Reduce the heat to low and add the shredded cheddar cheese and grated Parmesan cheese. Stir until melted and smooth.
    5. Season with salt, pepper, paprika, and garlic powder, if using.
    6. Add the cooked macaroni pasta to the cheese sauce, stirring until well combined. Remove from heat and let cool slightly.

2. Form the Mac and Cheese Bites:

    1. Preheat your oven to 375°F (190°C). Grease a mini muffin tin with cooking spray or oil.
    2. Once the macaroni and cheese mixture has cooled enough to handle, take small scoops and roll them into balls, about 1-2 tablespoons each.
    3. Place each mac and cheese ball into the mini muffin tin, pressing gently to pack them in.

3. Coat and Bake the Bites:

    1. Set up a breading station with beaten eggs in one bowl and seasoned breadcrumbs in another.
    2. Dip each mac and cheese ball first into the beaten eggs, coating evenly.

3. Then, roll the coated ball in the seasoned breadcrumbs, pressing gently to adhere.
4. Place the coated mac and cheese bites back into the mini muffin tin.

4. Bake:

1. Bake in the preheated oven for 20-25 minutes, or until the bites are golden brown and crispy on the outside.

5. Serve:

1. Allow the mac and cheese bites to cool slightly before carefully removing them from the muffin tin.
2. Serve warm as an appetizer or snack. They can be enjoyed plain or with a side of marinara sauce, ranch dressing, or your favorite dipping sauce.

Tips:

- Cheese Variations: Feel free to experiment with different cheeses like mozzarella, Gruyère, or Monterey Jack for varied flavors.
- Make-Ahead: You can prepare the mac and cheese mixture ahead of time and assemble and bake the bites just before serving.
- Freezing: These mac and cheese bites can be frozen after baking. Reheat them in the oven until warmed through for a quick snack.

These mac and cheese bites are sure to be a hit at parties or as a fun snack for the family. Enjoy the creamy inside and crispy outside of these delightful bites!

Sausage Balls

Ingredients:

- 1 lb ground pork sausage (mild or hot, depending on your preference)
- 2 cups shredded cheddar cheese
- 1 1/2 cups biscuit mix (such as Bisquick)
- 1/4 cup milk
- 1/2 teaspoon garlic powder (optional)
- 1/2 teaspoon onion powder (optional)
- 1/4 teaspoon ground black pepper
- 1/4 teaspoon cayenne pepper (optional, for a bit of heat)
- Fresh parsley or chives, chopped (optional, for garnish)

Instructions:

1. Preheat Oven:

    1. Preheat your oven to 375°F (190°C). Line a baking sheet with parchment paper or lightly grease it.

2. Mix Ingredients:

    1. In a large mixing bowl, combine the ground pork sausage, shredded cheddar cheese, biscuit mix, milk, garlic powder, onion powder, black pepper, and cayenne pepper (if using).
    2. Mix everything together until well combined. It's easiest to mix with clean hands to ensure all ingredients are evenly distributed.

3. Form Sausage Balls:

    1. Take about 1 tablespoon of the mixture and roll it into a ball using your hands. Place each ball onto the prepared baking sheet.
    2. Repeat until all the mixture is used, spacing the sausage balls about 1 inch apart on the baking sheet.

4. Bake:

    1. Bake in the preheated oven for 18-20 minutes, or until the sausage balls are cooked through and golden brown on the outside.

5. Serve:

    1. Remove the sausage balls from the oven and let them cool slightly on the baking sheet.
    2. If desired, sprinkle chopped fresh parsley or chives over the sausage balls for garnish before serving.

6. Enjoy:

   1. Serve the sausage balls warm as an appetizer or snack. They can be enjoyed on their own or with a dipping sauce such as barbecue sauce, honey mustard, or ranch dressing.

Tips:

- Variations: Feel free to customize the sausage balls by using different types of cheese (like pepper jack for a kick) or adding additional seasonings to suit your taste.
- Make-Ahead: You can prepare the sausage ball mixture ahead of time and refrigerate it until you're ready to bake. This is convenient for parties or gatherings.
- Freezing: Sausage balls can be frozen after baking. To reheat, simply bake in a preheated oven until heated through.

These sausage balls are hearty, flavorful, and perfect for any occasion. They're especially great for game day gatherings or holiday parties. Enjoy the delicious combination of sausage and cheese in every bite!

Jalapeño Poppers

Ingredients:

- 12 fresh jalapeño peppers
- 8 oz cream cheese, softened
- 1 cup shredded cheddar cheese (or cheese blend of your choice)
- 1/2 teaspoon garlic powder
- 1/2 teaspoon onion powder
- 1/4 teaspoon paprika
- Salt and pepper, to taste
- 1 cup breadcrumbs (plain or seasoned)
- 2 eggs, beaten
- Cooking spray or oil, for greasing

Instructions:

1. Prepare the Jalapeños:

   1. Preheat your oven to 375°F (190°C). Line a baking sheet with parchment paper.
   2. Slice each jalapeño pepper in half lengthwise. Use a spoon to scoop out the seeds and membranes, creating a hollow cavity for the filling. Wear gloves if sensitive to spicy peppers and avoid touching your face.

2. Make the Filling:

   1. In a mixing bowl, combine the softened cream cheese, shredded cheddar cheese, garlic powder, onion powder, paprika, salt, and pepper. Mix until well combined.
   2. Spoon or pipe the cheese mixture into each jalapeño half, filling them evenly.

3. Bread the Jalapeño Poppers:

   1. Set up a breading station with beaten eggs in one bowl and breadcrumbs in another.
   2. Dip each filled jalapeño half into the beaten eggs, ensuring it's fully coated.
   3. Roll the egg-coated jalapeño in breadcrumbs, pressing gently to adhere.
   4. Place the breaded jalapeño poppers on the prepared baking sheet.

4. Bake the Jalapeño Poppers:

   1. Lightly spray or brush the tops of the jalapeño poppers with cooking spray or oil to help them brown.
   2. Bake in the preheated oven for 20-25 minutes, or until the jalapeños are tender and the filling is melted and bubbly, and the breadcrumbs are golden brown.

5. Serve:

1. Remove the jalapeño poppers from the oven and let them cool slightly before serving.
2. Serve warm as an appetizer or snack. They can be enjoyed on their own or with a dipping sauce like ranch dressing, sour cream, or salsa.

Tips:

- Spice Level: Adjust the heat of the jalapeño poppers by removing more or less of the seeds and membranes. Leaving some seeds will make them spicier.
- Variations: Add cooked and crumbled bacon, diced green onions, or chopped cilantro to the cheese mixture for added flavor.
- Frying Option: Instead of baking, you can also fry the breaded jalapeño poppers in hot oil until golden brown and crispy.

Jalapeño poppers are a delightful treat that combines creamy, cheesy goodness with a bit of heat from the jalapeños. They're perfect for parties, game days, or anytime you crave a spicy appetizer!

Tater Tots

Ingredients:

- 2 lbs russet potatoes (about 4 medium potatoes)
- 1 teaspoon salt
- 1/2 teaspoon garlic powder
- 1/2 teaspoon onion powder
- 1/4 teaspoon paprika
- 1/4 teaspoon black pepper
- 1/4 cup all-purpose flour
- Cooking oil, for frying (such as vegetable oil or canola oil)
- Optional: ketchup, ranch dressing, or other dipping sauces for serving

Instructions:

1. Prepare the Potatoes:

   1. Peel the potatoes and cut them into chunks. Place them in a large pot and cover with cold water. Add 1 teaspoon of salt to the water.
   2. Bring the water to a boil over medium-high heat. Cook the potatoes until they are fork-tender, about 15-20 minutes.
   3. Drain the potatoes and let them cool slightly.

2. Mash and Season the Potatoes:

   1. Mash the cooked potatoes using a potato masher or fork until smooth and lump-free.
   2. Add the garlic powder, onion powder, paprika, black pepper, and flour to the mashed potatoes. Mix well until everything is evenly combined.

3. Form the Tater Tots:

   1. Take small portions of the potato mixture and roll them into small cylindrical shapes, about 1 inch long and 1/2 inch thick. Repeat until all the mixture is used, placing the formed tater tots on a baking sheet lined with parchment paper.

4. Fry the Tater Tots:

   1. In a large skillet or frying pan, heat about 1/2 inch of cooking oil over medium-high heat until hot (around 350°F or 175°C).
   2. Carefully place the tater tots into the hot oil in batches, making sure not to overcrowd the pan. Fry them for about 2-3 minutes per side, or until they are golden brown and crispy.
   3. Remove the fried tater tots from the oil using a slotted spoon or tongs and place them on a plate lined with paper towels to drain excess oil.

5. Serve:

1. Serve the homemade tater tots hot and crispy, optionally with ketchup, ranch dressing, or your favorite dipping sauce on the side.

Tips:

- Baking Option: If you prefer a healthier option, you can bake the tater tots instead of frying them. Preheat your oven to 425°F (220°C), place the formed tater tots on a baking sheet lined with parchment paper, and bake for about 25-30 minutes, turning halfway through, until golden and crispy.
- Freezing: You can freeze uncooked tater tots on a baking sheet until solid, then transfer them to a freezer bag for longer storage. Fry or bake them directly from frozen, adding a few extra minutes to the cooking time.

Homemade tater tots are a fun and delicious way to enjoy crispy potato goodness at home. They're great as a snack, side dish, or even as a party appetizer!

Chocolate Covered Pretzels

Ingredients:

- 1 bag (10-12 oz) of pretzels (mini pretzels or large pretzel rods)
- 8 oz semi-sweet chocolate, chopped (or chocolate chips)
- 8 oz white chocolate, chopped (optional, for drizzling)
- Sprinkles, crushed nuts, or other toppings (optional)

Instructions:

1. Prepare the Pretzels:

    1. Line a baking sheet with parchment paper or wax paper.
    2. If using pretzel rods, break them in half for easier handling.

2. Melt the Chocolate:

    1. Place the semi-sweet chocolate in a microwave-safe bowl. Microwave in 30-second intervals, stirring after each interval, until the chocolate is melted and smooth.
    2. If using white chocolate for drizzling, melt it in a separate bowl using the same method.

3. Dip the Pretzels:

    1. Using a fork or a dipping tool, dip each pretzel into the melted semi-sweet chocolate, coating it halfway or fully as desired.
    2. Gently tap the fork against the side of the bowl to remove excess chocolate.
    3. Place the dipped pretzels on the prepared baking sheet. If adding toppings like sprinkles or crushed nuts, sprinkle them onto the chocolate while it's still wet.

4. Drizzle with White Chocolate (optional):

    1. Once the semi-sweet chocolate has set (you can speed up the process by placing the baking sheet in the refrigerator for a few minutes), drizzle the melted white chocolate over the pretzels using a spoon or a fork.

5. Let the Chocolate Set:

    1. Allow the chocolate covered pretzels to sit at room temperature until the chocolate is completely set and hardened.

6. Serve or Store:

    1. Once the chocolate is set, transfer the chocolate covered pretzels to an airtight container for storage.

2. Enjoy your homemade chocolate covered pretzels as a sweet and salty snack or as a delicious treat for parties and gatherings!

Tips:

- Variations: Experiment with different types of chocolate such as milk chocolate or dark chocolate. You can also use flavored chocolates or add extracts like peppermint or almond to the melted chocolate for extra flavor.
- Decoration: Besides sprinkles and crushed nuts, you can also drizzle caramel sauce or peanut butter over the chocolate covered pretzels for added indulgence.
- Storage: Store chocolate covered pretzels in an airtight container at room temperature. They should stay fresh for about a week, but they're usually eaten much quicker!

Making chocolate covered pretzels at home is a fun and rewarding activity, and they make wonderful homemade gifts too. Enjoy the combination of crunchy pretzels and smooth, rich chocolate in every bite!

Fruit Platter

Ingredients:

- Assorted fresh fruits such as:
    - Strawberries
    - Grapes (green, red, or both)
    - Pineapple chunks
    - Watermelon slices or cubes
    - Cantaloupe or honeydew melon balls or slices
    - Blueberries
    - Raspberries or blackberries
    - Kiwi slices
    - Oranges or mandarin segments
- Optional: Fresh mint leaves for garnish

Instructions:

1. Prepare the Fruits:

    1. Wash all the fruits thoroughly under cold water. Pat them dry with paper towels.
    2. Prepare the fruits by cutting them into bite-sized pieces or slices as needed. For example, slice strawberries, cut pineapple into chunks, peel and slice kiwi, etc.

2. Arrange the Fruit Platter:

    1. Start by choosing a large platter or serving board that will comfortably fit all the fruits.
    2. Begin arranging the fruits in groups or sections, creating an attractive and balanced presentation. You can arrange them in rows, concentric circles, or any pattern you prefer.
    3. Place larger fruits like melon slices or pineapple chunks around the edges or corners of the platter to anchor the display.
    4. Fill in the gaps with smaller fruits like berries to add color and texture.

3. Garnish (Optional):

    1. If desired, garnish the fruit platter with fresh mint leaves scattered over the top. This adds a touch of greenery and freshness.

4. Serve:

    1. Serve the fruit platter immediately, or cover it with plastic wrap and refrigerate until ready to serve. If refrigerated, bring the fruit platter to room temperature for about 15-20 minutes before serving for the best flavor.

5. Tips for Serving:

1. Provide small forks or toothpicks for easy serving, especially if the fruits are cut into bite-sized pieces.
2. Consider adding a small bowl of yogurt, honey, or a fruit dip on the side for dipping.
3. Customize the fruit selection based on seasonal availability and personal preferences. Use a variety of colors and textures for an appealing presentation.
4. Leftovers can be stored in an airtight container in the refrigerator and enjoyed within a few days.

A well-arranged fruit platter not only looks inviting but also provides a healthy and refreshing option for any occasion. It's a versatile dish that complements breakfast, brunch, lunch, or as a light dessert option after a meal.

Veggie Platter

Ingredients:

- Assorted fresh vegetables such as:
    - Cherry tomatoes
    - Baby carrots
    - Cucumber slices
    - Bell pepper strips (various colors)
    - Celery sticks
    - Broccoli florets
    - Cauliflower florets
    - Snap peas or sugar snap peas
    - Radishes
    - Mini sweet peppers
- Optional: Fresh herbs for garnish (parsley, cilantro, etc.)

Instructions:

1. Prepare the Vegetables:

   1. Wash all the vegetables thoroughly under cold water. Pat them dry with paper towels.
   2. Prepare the vegetables by cutting them into bite-sized pieces or strips as needed. For example, halve cherry tomatoes, slice cucumbers and bell peppers, cut celery into sticks, etc.

2. Arrange the Veggie Platter:

   1. Choose a large platter or serving board that will comfortably fit all the vegetables.
   2. Start arranging the vegetables in groups or sections, creating a visually appealing and balanced presentation. You can arrange them in rows, concentric circles, or any pattern you prefer.
   3. Place larger vegetables like cherry tomatoes or bell pepper strips around the edges or corners of the platter to anchor the display.
   4. Fill in the gaps with smaller vegetables like baby carrots or snap peas to add variety.

3. Garnish (Optional):

   1. If desired, garnish the veggie platter with fresh herbs such as parsley or cilantro scattered over the top. This adds a touch of color and freshness.

4. Serve:

1. Serve the veggie platter immediately, or cover it with plastic wrap and refrigerate until ready to serve. If refrigerated, bring the veggie platter to room temperature for about 15-20 minutes before serving.

5. Tips for Serving:

1. Provide small bowls of hummus, ranch dressing, or another favorite dip in the center or around the platter for dipping.
2. Customize the vegetable selection based on seasonal availability and personal preferences. Use a variety of colors and textures for an appealing presentation.
3. Leftovers can be stored in an airtight container in the refrigerator and enjoyed within a few days.

A well-arranged veggie platter not only looks inviting but also provides a nutritious and delicious option for any occasion. It's a versatile dish that complements parties, picnics, or any gathering where you want to offer a healthy snack or appetizer.

Cheese and Crackers

Ingredients:

- Assorted cheeses (choose a variety of flavors and textures):
    - Sharp cheddar
    - Brie
    - Gouda
    - Blue cheese
    - Goat cheese (chevre)
    - Swiss
    - Pepper jack
    - Manchego
- Assorted crackers or crispbreads:
    - Water crackers
    - Wheat crackers
    - Rye crackers
    - Multigrain crackers
    - Pita chips
    - Baguette slices (toasted or untoasted)
- Optional accompaniments:
    - Sliced cured meats (such as salami or prosciutto)
    - Fresh fruit (grapes, apple slices, pear slices)
    - Dried fruits (figs, apricots)
    - Nuts (almonds, walnuts)
    - Olives
    - Honey or fig jam for drizzling or spreading

Instructions:

1. Select and Prepare the Cheeses:

    1. Choose a selection of cheeses that vary in flavor and texture to provide a diverse tasting experience. Consider including both soft and hard cheeses.
    2. Arrange the cheeses on a large serving platter or board. You can either slice or cube the cheeses, depending on your preference.

2. Choose Crackers and Crispbreads:

    1. Select a variety of crackers and crispbreads that complement the cheeses. Arrange them on the platter or in separate bowls for easy access.

3. Arrange Accompaniments (Optional):

1. Place sliced cured meats, fresh and dried fruits, nuts, olives, and any other accompaniments around the cheeses and crackers on the platter. This adds variety and enhances the flavor combinations.

4. Serve:

1. Serve the cheese and crackers platter at room temperature to allow the flavors of the cheeses to fully develop.
2. Encourage guests to mix and match different cheeses with crackers and accompaniments to create their own flavor combinations.
3. Provide small knives or cheese spreaders for guests to easily serve themselves.

Tips:

- Cheese Selection: Aim for a balance of flavors, textures, and colors when selecting cheeses. Include both familiar favorites and adventurous choices for variety.
- Presentation: Arrange the cheeses and crackers in an attractive and organized manner on the platter or board. Consider using garnishes like fresh herbs or edible flowers for an elegant touch.
- Customization: Tailor the cheese and crackers platter to suit your guests' preferences and dietary needs. Offer gluten-free crackers or vegan cheese alternatives if needed.
- Leftovers: Store any leftover cheeses and accompaniments separately in airtight containers in the refrigerator. Cheese can be enjoyed again within a few days.

A well-curated cheese and crackers platter not only satisfies appetites but also provides an interactive and enjoyable dining experience. It's a versatile option that can be enjoyed as an appetizer, a light meal, or a part of a larger spread.

Chicken Quesadillas

Ingredients:

- 2 cups cooked chicken, shredded or diced (rotisserie chicken works well)
- 1 cup shredded cheese (such as Mexican cheese blend, cheddar, or Monterey Jack)
- 1/2 cup diced bell peppers (any color you prefer)
- 1/4 cup diced red onion
- 1 teaspoon chili powder
- 1/2 teaspoon ground cumin
- 1/2 teaspoon garlic powder
- Salt and pepper, to taste
- 4 large flour tortillas (8 or 10-inch size)
- Cooking spray or butter, for cooking
- Optional toppings: salsa, sour cream, guacamole, chopped cilantro

Instructions:

1. Prepare the Chicken:

    1. If you haven't already cooked the chicken, you can cook chicken breasts or use leftover cooked chicken like rotisserie chicken. Shred or dice the chicken into bite-sized pieces.

2. Prepare the Filling:

    1. In a bowl, combine the cooked chicken, shredded cheese, diced bell peppers, diced red onion, chili powder, ground cumin, garlic powder, salt, and pepper. Mix well to combine all the ingredients.

3. Assemble the Quesadillas:

    1. Heat a large non-stick skillet or griddle over medium heat.
    2. Place one tortilla flat on the skillet. Spoon a quarter of the chicken mixture onto half of the tortilla, spreading it evenly.
    3. Fold the empty half of the tortilla over the filling, creating a half-moon shape.
    4. Press down gently with a spatula to flatten the quesadilla slightly.

4. Cook the Quesadillas:

    1. Cook the quesadilla for about 2-3 minutes on each side, or until the tortilla is golden brown and crispy, and the cheese is melted inside.
    2. Repeat with the remaining tortillas and chicken mixture, cooking one quesadilla at a time or as many as your skillet can comfortably hold.

5. Serve:

1. Remove the quesadillas from the skillet and let them cool slightly before cutting them into wedges or halves.
2. Serve hot with optional toppings such as salsa, sour cream, guacamole, and chopped cilantro.

Tips:

- Variations: Feel free to customize your quesadillas with additional ingredients like sliced jalapeños, black beans, corn, or different types of cheese.
- Cooking Tips: If you prefer a crispier quesadilla, you can brush the outside of the tortillas with a little melted butter or spray them with cooking spray before cooking.
- Storage: Quesadillas are best enjoyed fresh and hot off the skillet. If you have leftovers, store them in an airtight container in the refrigerator and reheat in a skillet or microwave.

Chicken quesadillas are a versatile dish that can be enjoyed as a quick lunch, dinner, or even as a party appetizer. They're sure to be a hit with their gooey cheese, flavorful chicken, and crispy tortilla exterior!

Meat and Cheese Platter

Ingredients:

Meats:

- Assorted cured meats such as:
    - Prosciutto
    - Salami (e.g., Genoa, Soppressata)
    - Pepperoni
    - Chorizo
    - Capicola
    - Ham (e.g., Serrano, Black Forest)

Cheeses:

- Assorted cheeses such as:
    - Brie
    - Gouda
    - Manchego
    - Blue cheese (e.g., Gorgonzola, Roquefort)
    - Cheddar (sharp or aged)
    - Goat cheese (chevre)
    - Swiss (e.g., Gruyère, Emmental)

Accompaniments:

- Crackers or breadsticks
- Fresh fruit (grapes, figs, apple slices)
- Dried fruit (apricots, figs)
- Nuts (almonds, walnuts)
- Olives (various types)
- Pickles or gherkins
- Honey or fig jam

Optional Garnishes:

- Fresh herbs (rosemary sprigs, thyme)
- Edible flowers (for a decorative touch)

Instructions:

1. Prepare the Meats and Cheeses:

    1. Arrange the cured meats on a large serving platter or wooden board, folding or rolling them for an attractive presentation.

2. Cut the cheeses into slices, wedges, or cubes. Arrange them on the platter alongside the meats.

2. Arrange the Accompaniments:

   1. Place crackers or breadsticks in between the meats and cheeses on the platter.
   2. Distribute fresh and dried fruits, nuts, olives, pickles, and any other accompaniments around the meats and cheeses.

3. Optional Garnishes:

   1. If desired, garnish the platter with fresh herbs or edible flowers for a decorative touch.

4. Serve:

   1. Serve the meat and cheese platter at room temperature to allow the flavors to fully develop.
   2. Provide small knives or cheese spreaders for guests to easily serve themselves.
   3. Encourage guests to mix and match different meats and cheeses with the accompaniments for a variety of flavor combinations.

Tips:

- Variety: Aim for a balance of flavors, textures, and colors when selecting meats, cheeses, and accompaniments. Include both mild and bold flavors for a diverse tasting experience.
- Presentation: Arrange the meats and cheeses in an aesthetically pleasing manner on the platter or board. Consider using small bowls or ramekins for olives, honey, or jams to prevent them from spreading on the board.
- Customization: Tailor the meat and cheese platter to suit your guests' preferences and dietary needs. Offer gluten-free crackers or vegan cheese alternatives if needed.
- Storage: Store any leftover meats and cheeses separately in the refrigerator. They can be enjoyed within a few days, but charcuterie platters are best enjoyed fresh.

A well-curated meat and cheese platter not only provides a delicious assortment of flavors but also serves as an elegant centerpiece for any gathering. It's a versatile option that can be served as an appetizer, a light meal, or a part of a larger spread.

Hummus

Ingredients:

- 1 can (15 oz) chickpeas (garbanzo beans), drained and rinsed
- 1/4 cup tahini (sesame paste)
- 3 tablespoons lemon juice (from about 1 large lemon)
- 1-2 cloves garlic, minced
- 2-3 tablespoons extra virgin olive oil
- 1/2 teaspoon ground cumin
- Salt, to taste
- Water, as needed for desired consistency
- Optional garnishes: Extra olive oil, paprika, chopped fresh parsley, pine nuts

Instructions:

1. Prepare the Chickpeas:

   1. Drain and rinse the chickpeas under cold water. Remove any loose skins by gently rubbing them between your fingers (optional, but it can result in smoother hummus).

2. Make the Hummus:

   1. In a food processor or blender, combine the chickpeas, tahini, lemon juice, minced garlic, olive oil, ground cumin, and a pinch of salt.
   2. Process the mixture until smooth and creamy. Scrape down the sides of the processor bowl or blender as needed to ensure all ingredients are well combined.
   3. If the hummus is too thick, gradually add water, 1 tablespoon at a time, until you reach your desired creamy consistency.
   4. Taste and adjust seasoning by adding more salt or lemon juice if needed.

3. Serve:

   1. Transfer the hummus to a serving bowl. Create a swirl on the surface with the back of a spoon and drizzle with a little extra virgin olive oil.
   2. Optionally, sprinkle with paprika, chopped fresh parsley, or pine nuts for garnish.
   3. Serve hummus with pita bread, crackers, fresh vegetables (carrots, cucumbers, bell peppers), or use it as a spread in sandwiches and wraps.

Tips:

- Variations: You can customize your hummus by adding roasted red peppers, sun-dried tomatoes, olives, or fresh herbs like cilantro or basil during blending for different flavors.
- Storage: Store homemade hummus in an airtight container in the refrigerator. It will keep well for about 4-5 days. Stir before serving if any separation occurs.

- Texture: For an extra smooth hummus, you can peel the chickpeas after rinsing by gently pinching them to remove the skins. This step is optional but can enhance the texture.
- Make-Ahead: Hummus can be made ahead of time and stored in the refrigerator until ready to serve. It's great for meal prep or for entertaining guests.

Homemade hummus is nutritious, flavorful, and incredibly versatile. Whether as a healthy snack, a party dip, or part of a meal, it's sure to be a crowd-pleaser with its creamy texture and rich, nutty taste.

Roasted Chickpeas

Ingredients:

- 1 can (15 oz) chickpeas (garbanzo beans), drained and rinsed
- 1-2 tablespoons olive oil
- 1 teaspoon ground cumin
- 1/2 teaspoon smoked paprika (optional, for added flavor)
- 1/2 teaspoon garlic powder
- 1/2 teaspoon salt, or to taste
- Freshly ground black pepper, to taste

Instructions:

1. Preheat the Oven:

    1. Preheat your oven to 400°F (200°C).

2. Prepare the Chickpeas:

    1. Drain and rinse the chickpeas thoroughly under cold water. Pat them dry with a clean kitchen towel or paper towels. Removing excess moisture helps in achieving crispy roasted chickpeas.

3. Season the Chickpeas:

    1. In a mixing bowl, toss the dried chickpeas with olive oil until evenly coated.
    2. Add ground cumin, smoked paprika (if using), garlic powder, salt, and black pepper to the chickpeas. Toss again until the chickpeas are coated with the seasonings.

4. Roast the Chickpeas:

    1. Spread the seasoned chickpeas in a single layer on a baking sheet lined with parchment paper or a silicone baking mat.
    2. Roast in the preheated oven for 25-30 minutes, shaking the pan halfway through baking, until the chickpeas are crispy and golden brown. Keep an eye on them towards the end to prevent burning.

5. Cool and Serve:

    1. Remove the roasted chickpeas from the oven and let them cool slightly on the baking sheet. They will crisp up further as they cool.
    2. Serve the roasted chickpeas warm or at room temperature as a snack. They can also be stored in an airtight container at room temperature for a few days.

Tips:

- Variations: Feel free to experiment with different seasonings such as chili powder, curry powder, Italian seasoning, or even a touch of cinnamon for sweet-spicy roasted chickpeas.
- Texture: For extra crunchy roasted chickpeas, you can bake them for a few additional minutes. Keep checking them to achieve your desired level of crispiness.
- Make-Ahead: Roasted chickpeas are best enjoyed fresh for optimal crunchiness. If they lose their crispiness, you can reheat them in a low oven for a few minutes to revive their texture.
- Uses: Enjoy roasted chickpeas as a snack on their own, or use them as a crunchy topping for salads, soups, or yogurt bowls. They also make a great addition to charcuterie boards or as a garnish for various dishes.

Roasted chickpeas are not only delicious but also packed with protein and fiber, making them a healthy alternative to traditional snacks. They're perfect for satisfying cravings while providing a satisfying crunch!

Fried Pickles

Ingredients:

- 1 jar of dill pickle slices or spears (about 16 oz)
- 1 cup buttermilk
- 1 cup all-purpose flour
- 1 teaspoon garlic powder
- 1 teaspoon paprika
- 1/2 teaspoon cayenne pepper (optional, for a bit of heat)
- Salt and pepper, to taste
- Vegetable oil, for frying
- Ranch dressing or your favorite dipping sauce, for serving

Instructions:

1. Prepare the Pickles:

    1. Drain the pickles from the jar and pat them dry with paper towels. Excess moisture will prevent the breading from sticking.

2. Set Up Dredging Station:

    1. In a shallow bowl, pour the buttermilk.
    2. In another shallow bowl, combine the flour, garlic powder, paprika, cayenne pepper (if using), salt, and pepper. Mix well to combine the dry ingredients.

3. Bread the Pickles:

    1. Heat vegetable oil in a large skillet or frying pan over medium-high heat until it reaches about 350°F (175°C). You want enough oil to submerge the pickles halfway.
    2. Dip each pickle slice or spear into the buttermilk, allowing any excess to drip off.
    3. Coat the pickle thoroughly in the seasoned flour mixture, pressing gently to adhere the coating.

4. Fry the Pickles:

    1. Carefully place the breaded pickles in the hot oil, in batches if necessary to avoid overcrowding the pan.
    2. Fry for about 2-3 minutes per side, or until they are golden brown and crispy. Use tongs or a slotted spoon to turn them halfway through cooking.
    3. Once fried, remove the pickles from the oil and place them on a plate lined with paper towels to drain excess oil.

5. Serve:

1. Arrange the fried pickles on a serving platter and serve them hot with ranch dressing or your favorite dipping sauce on the side.

Tips:

- Variations: You can add different seasonings to the flour mixture, such as onion powder, smoked paprika, or Italian seasoning, to customize the flavor of your fried pickles.
- Double Coating: For an extra crispy texture, you can double coat the pickles by dipping them back into the buttermilk and then the flour mixture again before frying.
- Oven Baked Option: If you prefer a healthier alternative, you can bake the breaded pickles in a preheated oven at 425°F (220°C) on a baking sheet lined with parchment paper. Spray the pickles with cooking spray and bake for about 15-20 minutes, flipping halfway through, until crispy and golden brown.
- Storage: Fried pickles are best enjoyed fresh and hot. If you have leftovers, store them in an airtight container in the refrigerator. Reheat them in the oven to crisp them up again before serving.

Fried pickles are a crunchy and flavorful snack that's perfect for parties, game nights, or anytime you're craving a unique appetizer. Enjoy the tangy bite of the pickles contrasted with the crispy coating!

Baked Zucchini Chips

Ingredients:

- 2 medium zucchini, thinly sliced (about 1/8 inch thick rounds)
- 2 tablespoons olive oil
- 1/4 cup grated Parmesan cheese
- 1/4 cup breadcrumbs (plain or seasoned)
- 1/2 teaspoon garlic powder
- 1/2 teaspoon dried oregano
- 1/2 teaspoon paprika (optional, for added flavor)
- Salt and pepper, to taste

Instructions:

1. Preheat the Oven:

    1. Preheat your oven to 425°F (220°C). Line a baking sheet with parchment paper or lightly grease it with olive oil.

2. Prepare the Zucchini:

    1. Wash the zucchini thoroughly and slice them into thin rounds, about 1/8 inch thick. Pat the slices dry with a clean kitchen towel or paper towels to remove excess moisture.

3. Prepare the Coating Mixture:

    1. In a shallow bowl, combine the grated Parmesan cheese, breadcrumbs, garlic powder, dried oregano, paprika (if using), salt, and pepper. Mix well to combine.

4. Coat the Zucchini Slices:

    1. Brush each zucchini slice lightly with olive oil on both sides.
    2. Dip each slice into the breadcrumb mixture, pressing gently to coat both sides evenly. Place the coated slices on the prepared baking sheet in a single layer, leaving a little space between each slice.

5. Bake the Zucchini Chips:

    1. Bake in the preheated oven for 15-20 minutes, or until the zucchini chips are golden brown and crispy. Flip the chips halfway through baking to ensure even cooking.
    2. Keep an eye on them towards the end of baking to prevent burning, as oven temperatures can vary.

6. Serve:

1. Remove the baked zucchini chips from the oven and let them cool slightly on the baking sheet.
2. Transfer the chips to a serving platter and serve them warm as a healthy snack or appetizer.

Tips:

- Slice Thickness: Try to slice the zucchini uniformly to ensure even baking. Thicker slices may require longer baking time, while thinner slices will cook more quickly.
- Seasoning Variations: Feel free to experiment with different seasonings such as Italian seasoning, cayenne pepper, or lemon zest for added flavor.
- Storage: Baked zucchini chips are best enjoyed fresh for optimal crispiness. If you have leftovers, store them in an airtight container at room temperature. Reheat them in the oven briefly to restore their crispiness before serving.
- Dipping Sauces: Serve baked zucchini chips with your favorite dipping sauce such as marinara sauce, ranch dressing, or tzatziki for added enjoyment.

Baked zucchini chips are a nutritious and satisfying snack that's low in calories and high in flavor. They're a great way to enjoy zucchini and satisfy cravings for crispy snacks without the guilt!

Soft Pretzels

Ingredients:

- 1 and 1/2 cups warm water (110-115°F)
- 1 tablespoon granulated sugar
- 2 teaspoons active dry yeast
- 4 cups all-purpose flour
- 1/2 teaspoon salt
- 2 tablespoons unsalted butter, melted
- Cooking spray or vegetable oil, for greasing
- 10 cups water
- 2/3 cup baking soda
- Coarse salt, for sprinkling

Instructions:

1. Activate the Yeast:

   1. In a large bowl or the bowl of a stand mixer, combine the warm water and sugar. Sprinkle the yeast over the top and let it sit for 5-10 minutes, until foamy.

2. Mix the Dough:

   1. Add the flour, salt, and melted butter to the yeast mixture. Mix until the dough comes together. If using a stand mixer, knead the dough with a dough hook attachment on medium speed for about 5 minutes. If kneading by hand, knead the dough on a lightly floured surface for about 7-8 minutes until smooth and elastic.
   2. Shape the dough into a ball and place it in a greased bowl, turning once to coat. Cover the bowl with a clean kitchen towel or plastic wrap and let the dough rise in a warm place for about 1 hour, or until doubled in size.

3. Preheat the Oven:

   1. Preheat your oven to 450°F (230°C). Line a baking sheet with parchment paper and lightly grease it with cooking spray or vegetable oil.

4. Prepare the Baking Soda Bath:

   1. In a large pot, bring 10 cups of water to a boil. Carefully add the baking soda (it will fizz up) and reduce the heat to simmer.

5. Shape the Pretzels:

   1. Punch down the risen dough and divide it into 8 equal pieces. Roll each piece into a long rope, about 20-22 inches long.

2. To shape each pretzel, form the rope into a U shape. Cross the ends over each other twice, then fold the ends down to form the classic pretzel shape. Press the ends into the bottom of the U to seal.

6. Boil the Pretzels:

    1. Carefully place each shaped pretzel, one or two at a time, into the simmering water bath for about 30 seconds. Use a slotted spoon or spatula to flip the pretzel halfway through. Remove the pretzel from the water and place it on the prepared baking sheet.

7. Bake the Pretzels:

    1. Sprinkle each pretzel with coarse salt while still wet from the water bath.
    2. Bake the pretzels in the preheated oven for 12-14 minutes, or until they are golden brown and cooked through. Rotate the baking sheet halfway through baking for even browning.

8. Serve:

    1. Remove the pretzels from the oven and let them cool slightly on a wire rack.
    2. Serve warm with mustard, cheese sauce, or your favorite dip.

Tips:

- Toppings: Besides coarse salt, you can sprinkle the pretzels with sesame seeds, poppy seeds, or even cinnamon sugar for a sweet variation.
- Storage: Soft pretzels are best enjoyed fresh on the day they are made. However, you can store leftovers in an airtight container at room temperature for up to 2 days. Reheat them in the oven to refresh their texture.
- Variations: Experiment with different shapes such as pretzel sticks or pretzel bites for bite-sized snacks.

Homemade soft pretzels are a fun and delicious baking project that yields impressive results. Enjoy them as a snack, appetizer, or even a special treat for gatherings or game nights!

Caprese Skewers

Ingredients:

- Cherry or grape tomatoes
- Fresh mozzarella balls (bocconcini)
- Fresh basil leaves
- Balsamic glaze or balsamic reduction
- Extra virgin olive oil
- Salt and freshly ground black pepper, to taste
- Wooden or bamboo skewers

Instructions:

1. Prepare the Ingredients:

    1. Rinse the cherry or grape tomatoes and pat them dry with paper towels. If using larger tomatoes, cut them into bite-sized pieces.
    2. Drain the fresh mozzarella balls (bocconcini) if they are stored in liquid.
    3. Rinse the fresh basil leaves and gently pat them dry with paper towels.

2. Assemble the Skewers:

    1. To assemble each skewer, thread a cherry tomato (or tomato piece) onto the skewer.
    2. Follow with a fresh mozzarella ball (bocconcini) and then a basil leaf. Repeat this pattern until the skewer is filled, leaving a little space at the end for easy handling.
    3. Continue assembling the remaining skewers until all ingredients are used.

3. Season and Serve:

    1. Arrange the Caprese skewers on a serving platter or board.
    2. Drizzle extra virgin olive oil and balsamic glaze or reduction over the skewers.
    3. Season with salt and freshly ground black pepper, to taste.

4. Serve:

    1. Serve the Caprese skewers immediately as a colorful and flavorful appetizer.

Tips:

- Variations: You can add a twist to your Caprese skewers by including grilled vegetables such as zucchini or bell peppers, or by adding a drizzle of pesto sauce for extra flavor.
- Presentation: Arrange the skewers on a bed of fresh arugula or mixed greens for an elegant presentation.

- Make-Ahead: You can prepare the individual components (tomatoes, mozzarella, and basil) ahead of time and assemble the skewers just before serving to keep them fresh.
- Storage: Caprese skewers are best served fresh. If you have leftovers, store them in an airtight container in the refrigerator for up to a day. Note that basil leaves may wilt if stored for too long.

Caprese skewers are not only visually appealing but also a delightful combination of flavors and textures that are sure to impress your guests at any gathering or party. Enjoy the fresh taste of summer with this simple yet elegant appetizer!

Chicken Satay

Ingredients:

For the Chicken Satay:

- 1 lb chicken breast or thigh meat, cut into thin strips or small cubes
- Wooden or bamboo skewers, soaked in water for 30 minutes (to prevent burning)
- 2 tablespoons vegetable oil, for grilling

For the Marinade:

- 1/4 cup coconut milk
- 1 tablespoon soy sauce
- 1 tablespoon fish sauce
- 1 tablespoon brown sugar
- 1 tablespoon curry powder
- 2 cloves garlic, minced
- 1 teaspoon ground turmeric (optional, for color)
- 1 teaspoon ground coriander
- 1/2 teaspoon ground cumin
- 1/4 teaspoon ground white pepper

For the Peanut Sauce:

- 1/2 cup smooth peanut butter
- 1/4 cup coconut milk
- 2 tablespoons soy sauce
- 1 tablespoon brown sugar
- 1 tablespoon lime juice
- 1 teaspoon minced fresh ginger
- 1 clove garlic, minced
- 1/2 teaspoon red pepper flakes (adjust to taste)
- Water, as needed to thin the sauce

Optional Garnish:

- Chopped peanuts
- Fresh cilantro or parsley, chopped
- Lime wedges

Instructions:

1. Marinate the Chicken:

1. In a bowl, whisk together all the marinade ingredients: coconut milk, soy sauce, fish sauce, brown sugar, curry powder, garlic, turmeric (if using), coriander, cumin, and white pepper.
2. Add the chicken strips or cubes to the marinade, ensuring they are well coated. Cover and refrigerate for at least 30 minutes, or up to 2 hours for more flavor.

2. Prepare the Peanut Sauce:

1. In a small saucepan over medium heat, combine the peanut butter, coconut milk, soy sauce, brown sugar, lime juice, minced ginger, garlic, and red pepper flakes.
2. Stir continuously until the sauce is smooth and heated through. If the sauce is too thick, add water a little at a time until you reach your desired consistency. Remove from heat and set aside.

3. Skewer and Grill the Chicken:

1. Preheat your grill or grill pan over medium-high heat. Brush with vegetable oil to prevent sticking.
2. Thread the marinated chicken onto the soaked skewers, shaking off any excess marinade.
3. Grill the chicken skewers for about 3-4 minutes per side, or until they are cooked through and have nice grill marks. Cooking time may vary depending on the thickness of your chicken pieces.

4. Serve:

1. Arrange the grilled chicken satay skewers on a serving platter.
2. Serve warm with the prepared peanut sauce on the side.
3. Garnish with chopped peanuts, fresh cilantro or parsley, and lime wedges if desired.

Tips:

- Alternative Cooking Methods: If you don't have a grill, you can also cook the chicken satay skewers under the broiler in your oven or on a stovetop grill pan.
- Make-Ahead: You can prepare the chicken marinade and peanut sauce ahead of time. Marinate the chicken and store it in the refrigerator until ready to grill. Reheat the peanut sauce gently before serving.
- Side Dishes: Chicken satay pairs well with steamed rice, cucumber salad, or Thai-style jasmine rice.
- Adjust Seasoning: Feel free to adjust the seasonings in both the marinade and peanut sauce to suit your taste preferences. Add more or less spice as desired.

Chicken satay is a delicious and satisfying dish that's perfect as an appetizer, main course, or party snack. Enjoy the tender, flavorful chicken with the rich and creamy peanut sauce for a taste of Southeast Asia at home!

Greek Yogurt Dip

Ingredients:

- 1 cup Greek yogurt (plain, full-fat or low-fat)
- 1 tablespoon fresh lemon juice
- 1 clove garlic, minced (optional, for a bit of kick)
- 1 tablespoon extra virgin olive oil
- 1 tablespoon chopped fresh dill (or 1 teaspoon dried dill)
- 1 tablespoon chopped fresh parsley
- Salt and pepper, to taste

Instructions:

1. Prepare the Greek Yogurt:

   1. In a medium bowl, combine the Greek yogurt and fresh lemon juice. Mix well until smooth.

2. Add Flavorings:

   1. Stir in the minced garlic (if using), extra virgin olive oil, chopped fresh dill, and chopped fresh parsley.
   2. Season with salt and pepper to taste. Mix thoroughly to combine all ingredients evenly.

3. Chill (Optional):

   1. For best flavor, cover the bowl with plastic wrap and refrigerate the dip for at least 30 minutes to allow the flavors to meld together. This step is optional but recommended.

4. Serve:

   1. Transfer the Greek yogurt dip to a serving bowl.
   2. Garnish with a drizzle of extra virgin olive oil and a sprig of fresh herbs (optional).
   3. Serve the dip with a variety of vegetables (carrots, cucumber, bell peppers), pita chips, or use it as a spread for sandwiches and wraps.

Tips:

- Variations: Feel free to customize the dip by adding other herbs such as mint, chives, or basil. You can also mix in finely chopped cucumber or grated cucumber for a refreshing tzatziki-style dip.
- Creaminess: Adjust the consistency by adding a small amount of water or more olive oil to achieve your desired thickness.

- Storage: Greek yogurt dip can be stored in an airtight container in the refrigerator for up to 3-4 days. Stir well before serving if any separation occurs.
- Healthier Option: Use low-fat or non-fat Greek yogurt for a lighter dip, or substitute with dairy-free yogurt alternatives for a vegan version.

This homemade Greek yogurt dip is creamy, tangy, and packed with fresh herbs and flavors. It's perfect for parties, picnics, or as a healthy snack option any time of the day!

Bacon-Wrapped Dates

Ingredients:

- 16 Medjool dates, pitted
- 8 slices of bacon, cut in half crosswise
- 16 whole almonds (optional, for stuffing)
- Toothpicks or wooden skewers

Instructions:

1. Preheat the Oven:

   1. Preheat your oven to 375°F (190°C). Line a baking sheet with parchment paper or aluminum foil for easy cleanup.

2. Prepare the Dates:

   1. If the dates are not already pitted, carefully make a lengthwise slit in each date and remove the pit.
   2. Optionally, stuff each date with a whole almond, inserting it into the cavity left by the pit.

3. Wrap with Bacon:

   1. Take a half-slice of bacon and wrap it around a stuffed date, securing it with a toothpick or skewer. Repeat with the remaining dates and bacon slices.

4. Bake the Bacon-Wrapped Dates:

   1. Arrange the bacon-wrapped dates on the prepared baking sheet, spaced apart to allow for even cooking.
   2. Bake in the preheated oven for 15-20 minutes, or until the bacon is crispy and cooked to your liking. You may want to flip the dates halfway through baking for even browning.

5. Serve:

   1. Once baked, remove the bacon-wrapped dates from the oven and let them cool slightly.
   2. Transfer to a serving platter and serve warm. Optionally, you can remove the toothpicks before serving, or leave them in for easy grabbing.

Tips:

- Variations: Instead of almonds, you can stuff the dates with other nuts such as pecans or walnuts, or even with cheese like blue cheese or goat cheese for added flavor.
- Sweeteners: If you prefer a sweeter version, you can drizzle honey or maple syrup over the bacon-wrapped dates before baking.

- Grilling Option: You can also grill bacon-wrapped dates on a preheated grill over medium heat until the bacon is crispy, turning occasionally to cook evenly.
- Presentation: Garnish with fresh herbs like parsley or chives for a pop of color and freshness.

Bacon-wrapped dates are a perfect appetizer for parties, gatherings, or even as a delicious snack any time. They offer a delightful combination of sweet, salty, and savory flavors that are sure to please your guests!

www.ingramcontent.com/pod-product-compliance
Lightning Source LLC
LaVergne TN
LVHW081600060526
838201LV00054B/1989